T0328594

Cambridge Elements ≡

Elements in Environmental Humanities
edited by
Louise Westling
University of Oregon
Serenella Iovino
University of North Carolina at Chapel Hill
Timo Maran
University of Tartu

CLIMATE CHANGE LITERACY

Julia Hoydis
University of Klagenfurt

Roman Bartosch
University of Cologne

Jens Martin Gurr
University of Duisburg-Essen

CAMBRIDGE
UNIVERSITY PRESS

Shaftesbury Road, Cambridge CB2 8EA, United Kingdom

One Liberty Plaza, 20th Floor, New York, NY 10006, USA

477 Williamstown Road, Port Melbourne, VIC 3207, Australia

314–321, 3rd Floor, Plot 3, Splendor Forum, Jasola District Centre, New Delhi – 110025, India

103 Penang Road, #05–06/07, Visioncrest Commercial, Singapore 238467

Cambridge University Press is part of Cambridge University Press & Assessment, a department of the University of Cambridge.

We share the University's mission to contribute to society through the pursuit of education, learning and research at the highest international levels of excellence.

www.cambridge.org
Information on this title: www.cambridge.org/9781009341998

DOI: 10.1017/9781009342032

First published 2023

A catalogue record for this publication is available from the British Library.

ISBN 978-1-009-34199-8 Paperback
ISSN 2632-3125 (online)
ISSN 2632-3117 (print)

Cambridge University Press & Assessment has no responsibility for the persistence or accuracy of URLs for external or third-party internet websites referred to in this publication and does not guarantee that any content on such websites is, or will remain, accurate or appropriate.

Climate Change Literacy

Elements in Environmental Humanities

DOI: 10.1017/9781009342032
First published online: May 2023

Julia Hoydis
University of Klagenfurt

Roman Bartosch
University of Cologne

Jens Martin Gurr
University of Duisburg-Essen

Author for correspondence: Roman Bartosch, roman.bartosch
@uni-koeln.de

Abstract: This Element presents a necessary intervention within the rapidly expanding field of research in the environmental humanities on climate change and environmental literacy. In contrast to the dominant, science-centred literacy debates, which largely ignore the unique resources of the humanities, it asks: How does literary reading contribute to climate change communication? How does this contribution relate to recent demands for environmental and related literacies? Rather than reducing the function of literature to a more pleasurable form of information transfer or its affective dimension of evoking sympathy, *Climate Change Literacy* thoroughly reassesses the cognitive, affective, and pedagogic potentials of literary writing. It does so by analysing a selection of popular climate novels and by demonstrating the role of fiction in fostering a more adequate understanding of, and response to, climate change. This title is also available as Open Access on Cambridge Core.

Keywords: Climate fiction, climate change communication, climate action, education for sustainability, critical literacy

ISBNs: 9781009341998 (PB), 9781009342032 (OC)
ISSNs: 2632-3125 (online), 2632-3117 (print)

Contents

Introduction

Clearly, reading novels won't save the planet. But facing the environmental crises we currently do, a case can and must be made that stories undoubtedly *do* matter and that literacy – essentially the ability to understand stories and make use of the transformative potential of this ability – matters greatly, too. Coming from literary studies and literature pedagogy, respectively, we therefore seek to (re-)assess the question of what literary reading might offer in response to the climate crisis and, in a second step, reflect on what this means for teaching literature.

Considering what one can only describe as three decades of failed public science communication about climate change (taking the first IPCC report in 1990 as a starting point) or, at best, as a communicative struggle that is yet to lead to any significant sociocultural and political change, it is now widely accepted that we need creative forms of communication – in other words, the arts and humanities have to come to the rescue of the hard sciences. Consequently, there's no shortage of artists and academics from all disciplines trying to communicate the global risks of climate change and doing amazing work in the process. They are united in the goal to 'promote storytelling as an entry point into a difficult and often emotionally charged conversation', as co-founder of the global Climate Change Theatre Action (CCTA) project, Chantal Bilodeau (2018, xv), notes. In the realm of anglophone literatures, so-called 'cli-fi', that is, the body of fictional and mostly speculative prose texts engaging with climate change as a main subject, has received particular attention as a rapidly growing field of artistic production and scholarly inquiry. Meanwhile, the urgency of the climate crisis is finally undeniable – even for most hardliner sceptics – and it is regularly making the news.

One of the reasons for this might be that climate change is increasingly visible on a global scale, including the affluent North, where disastrous storms, floods, and heatwaves are hitting at shorter intervals and with more disastrous consequences. It also has to do with related crises, such as alarming biodiversity loss and environmental injustices, not least intergenerationally. It is young people across the globe whose 'How dare you?' echoes through political and social debates on sustainability transformations and the threat of a perilous future ahead. In fact, current climatic developments surpass even the dire predictions and scenarios put forth by bodies such as the IPCC, with arctic ice melting faster, permafrost areas reaching dangerous tipping points quicker and species going extinct on a much broader scale than conservative estimates have projected. Finally, climate change has found its way into policy documents, curricula, and development strategies due to tireless activist campaigning and educational efforts to render it an issue of individual, communal, and global concern. A rhetoric of 'not here, not now' is being replaced by an understanding that catastrophes are indeed happening *here* (wherever this is, exactly) as well as *now* (however this temporal marker is conceptualised in the deep-time frame of what some call the Anthropocene).

Both developments – the physical realities hitting closer to home in ever more alarming severity, and the readiness to move from a general awareness of the situation to a realisation that individual, political, and global action is required – pertain to the ability to *read* climate change, and to read it *right*. For this reason, a better understanding of the scientific and cultural dimensions of climate change and its many related crises seems badly needed. But what makes for understanding the complex story and the cultural and scientific phenomenon that is climate change? While it has moved to the political agendas of parties, nations, and supra-national bodies, this question continues to concern scientists, scholars, and educators alike, who are thinking about, and making suggestions to tackle, the complexity and wickedness of climate change to bring about *appropriate* action. With each new concept of competent understanding and each new study of the impact of knowledge and awareness, it only becomes clearer that enabling people to read climate change demands cultural and educational innovation and mediation alongside, or even in fruitful tension with, scientific understanding.

This is not where the story ends, but where it begins. We agree with many working before and with us that it is especially important to become more competent and conversant with the cultural dimensions of climate change. Many scholars, in literary ecocriticism and elsewhere, as well as prominent authors of fiction have made the point that the current environmental crisis is also a crisis of the imagination (e.g., Buell 2005; Ghosh 2016). It pertains to metaphysics as well as physics; it touches on questions of ethics and values and the workings of human exceptionalism. It includes issues such as power, money, and societal organisation, especially economic and societal relations with the other-than-human world (see Plumwood 2002). Increasingly, it pertains to matters of complexity and conflict, also calling for humanities expertise in the 'diversity and mutability of historical conceptions of risk and value, opportunity and loss' (Garrard 2019, 4). While it is therefore hardly a new insight that the humanities are asked to aid with the gargantuan challenge of dealing with climate change, it seems time to readjust some of the current ideas concerning the role of literature and culture in this context, as well as some of the educational practices in the humanities and at all levels of formal education in English and elsewhere. This is what this Element seeks to do.

It is our conviction that literature can and ought to be a key element of climate education and action. But a more nuanced and comprehensive case must be made to sustain its value. This case needs to avoid reducing climate change to a 'problem' defined and construed according to a reductive protocol of scientific and solutionist thinking. Instead, it needs to think more and better about the idea that dramatic tipping points do not only exist in ecological earth-systems, but that there are also social tipping points towards sustainability and transformation that must be fuelled by research in the humanities. We take our cue from such research and agree that 'education to bolster understanding of the causes and effects of climate change, however important, will not be sufficient to transform society alone' (Otto et al. 2020, 2361). In other words, fostering climate *science* literacy through literature is not the subject of this Element. Although engagement with scientific 'facts' undoubtedly remains an important part of it, we endorse the claim that 'a purely science-oriented approach to climate change can miss the social, historical, ethical, and human realities that are critical to the problem. Climate change is an accelerator that exacerbates economic, racial, and social inequality' (Beach et al. 2017, 7). In what follows, we aim to add to the growing body of inspiring research on this subject in the environmental humanities and show that literary fiction has a crucial role to play in linking and exploring the scientific and social dimensions of anthropogenic climate change. It thus points to and allows for a better understanding of what we refer to as 'socio-ecological complexities', while fiction also imagines endings, creates space to confront loss and mourning, and dreams up alternative futures.

We frame this case for the value of literary reading about and amid climate change deliberately as one that requires joint efforts in the fields of literary studies and literature pedagogy. The former brings to the table an acute awareness of the specific nature of literary writing and the narratological toolkit that helps to describe it; the latter provides the pedagogical and methodological expertise in literacy (see Bartosch 2021). Specifically, we incorporate critical approaches from ecocriticism and education for sustainability, while also drawing on interdisciplinary research on the challenges of climate change communication. Here, psychological aspects of risk perception and decision-making are of special importance (see, e.g., Smith and Howe 2015, 7). For climate change, as Joe Smith explains, 'should not be responded to as a body of "facts" to be acted upon [. . .], but might instead be considered as a substantial and urgent collective risk management problem' (2011, 20). Adding to the familiar challenges of communicating risk – as human risk behaviour is never exclusively rational and instead framed by multiple cultural factors and 'feelings' and invariably expressed through narratives (see Hoydis 2019) – comes the matter of scales and complexity involved, creating a central barrier across lay–expert divides in climate change communication. Susanne C. Moser, herself an expert in this field, argues: 'Most individuals (even scientists) cannot and will never fully grasp and hold this amount of scientific complexity and uncertainty in their minds, much less be able to process it systematically' (2010, 35). Aside from the challenges this entails for climate change and literacy in science classrooms, it raises the question how literary reading works with perceptions and understandings of complexity and uncertainty – and if literary fiction can contribute something unique and valuable to it.

A productive approach to climate change literacy in the environmental humanities, we propose, is thus equally built on the specific potential and affordances of fiction *and* the methods and practices of education. 'Imagining climate futures, including the policies, technologies, behaviors, values and change processes that will take us there', writes Manjana Milkoreit, 'is something that we – our brains and our social technologies of imagination – *need to learn and practice*' (2016, 172; emphasis added). Highlighting the link between imagining climate futures and what we call 'literacy environments', we also seek to explore the 'possibility of strengthening our imagination skills' with the help of what Milkoreit calls 'an unusual tool: climate fiction' (Milkoreit 2016, 172). 'Cli-Fi', she explains, 'draws upon the full range of emotional, intellectual, philosophical, and spiritual capacities rather than appearing simply as a set of data points' (172). This is our cue – even though especially since the beginning of the 2020s, there has been a wide array of media on offer, including novels, film, video games, plays, and poetry, that could be assembled to make an even more encompassing case for the role of narrative in the context of climate change literacy. However, as scholars of literature, and especially the anglophone novel, we limit the focus to climate *prose* fiction, largely for two reasons. The first simply concerns scope and manageability, considering the sheer popularity of the emerging global body of cli-fi, including scholarly essays and monographs, empirical ecocritical studies in reader reception, and teaching suggestions and materials. The second reason follows from this: for the most part, we are working with concepts and ideas that have been developed in literary studies of prose narrative and cannot be transferred to other texts and forms of reader or viewer engagement without some heat loss. And yet, we hope that this Element will inform and inspire other educators and scholars to include and make strong cases for other media and their specific potentials in and beyond 'cli-fi'.

Apart from deciding to work with climate fiction novels rather than other ecomedia, we will have to say more below on our decision to work with a specific, and culturally rather narrow, selection of particularly popular exemplars of anglophone cli-fi. Idealist conceptions of the power of narrative are often based on interpretive assumptions of individual – and usually professional, academic – readers, typically a rather homogenous group. Aware of this inevitable bias, we have instead decided to draw on examples from a '"cli-fi" canon' that 'has emerged' and 'tended to dominate discussions', while at the same time, as Carl Death notes, 'the genre is growing rapidly' (2022, 445). We consciously avoid here the debates of whether or not 'cli-fi' can or should be considered a genre in its own right, the boundaries of the genre, and the tensions between speculation, realism, and apocalypse. Interesting as these questions might be to ecocritics, for the purpose of developing our notion of climate change literacy, we draw on popular examples of 'cli-fi' here, without seeking to limit the argument to a certain kind of text, or indeed medium – something we'll return to in the Afterword. The canon identified by Death and other scholars comprises texts by established authors such as Kim Stanley Robinson, Ian McEwan, Paolo Bacigalupi, Barbara Kingsolver, Saci Lloyd, and others, which are guaranteed a wide readership. There's also a strong correlation between scholarly attention and general popularity, as Matthew Schneider-Mayerson explains in his pioneering empirical study on 'the influence of climate fiction' (2018, 480). We are conscious, however, that the canon to date 'remains dominated by European and American perspectives and landscapes, often implicitly projecting a Western viewpoint as a global perspective' (Death 2022, 446; see also Nikoleris et al. 2017, 310). For this reason, in our 'Afterword' we will supplement these canonical texts with Afrofuturist and other fictions by authors from the Global South and include further reading suggestions. But primarily, and this needs stressing, this Element is theoretical in scope and does not recommend great 'cli-fi' books that mysteriously 'work', although that tends to be among the first questions one is inevitably asked when talking about this subject matter, as we've discovered on numerous occasions. Following ecocritic Greg Garrard, we can only reply that we have something to say about the value of reading and representations of climate change in literature, but that we do so, emphatically, 'without looking for the 'best''' (2012a, 199). This would imply the existence of a homogenous response to, and value assessment of, specific texts, which undermines a more general exploration of the value of literary reading. And it would solidify an inevitably exclusive canon. We are convinced that climate change literacy necessarily entails conflicting responses and listening to other stories than the popular and well-known ones. And yet, trying to better understand what popular texts – as literature – do, requires us to build our case for (teaching) the specific potential of literature on an empirically robust corpus of texts. This is why we take the selection as a starting point for our reflections, but bear in mind the need to eventually supplement these texts with more, and other, voices.

We are rehearsing our argument for a decidedly literary approach to climate change literacy because it resonates with urgent and vocal demands in climate change communication research to tap into the full potential of what communications scholar Maxwell Boykoff dubs 'creative communications'. Speaking of what he calls 'shared twenty-first-century communications ecosystems' (2019, xi), each with their own logics and responding publics, Boykoff criticises the prevalent concentration, in climate communication and elsewhere, on facts and figures in particular. Those mostly scientific and consensus-oriented ways of communication, Boykoff argues, fail at making present the realities of climate change for diverse audiences who, he avers, must be met where they are. We diverge in some respect from his suggestion to better involve feeling and affect, but we wholeheartedly agree that from the perspective of literacy research, 'there remains a dearth of systematic analyses regarding how creative climate communications elicit varying levels of awareness and engagement' (xi). However, it is not so much the creative ways of transmitting information and moving people into action that we are interested in, but the 'mental process of imagining [. . .] [as] a pre-condition for decision-making and political behavior' (Milkoreit 2016, 176). In other words, this Element explores what Schneider-Mayerson calls a 'fascinating theoretical question': 'what can literature and art do to move and inspire readers, and thereby contribute to efforts to respond to climate change, that other forms of communication don't?' (in Brady 2020). This stance towards narrative ways of communicating climate change eventually enables us to move beyond the field and concerns of climate communication research and the vexed question of finding the elusive *right* balance between messages (narratives) of hope and despair, between consolation and warning. It also speaks to a whole array of important work on narrative aesthetics and ethics or politics (as developed by W.C. Booth, Martha Nussbaum, and Jacques Rancière, for instance) outside of literary ecocriticism and education for sustainability, to which we will make some, though inevitably rather broad-brush, connections. In this Element, we will restrict our case to arguing that interpretively engaging with literature can foster climate change literacy and that this can be an important form of climate action in itself – and deserves to be discussed in its variety and potential.

Leaving the nascent field of empirical ecocriticism (see, e.g., Schneider-Mayerson et al. 2020) aside, when it comes to making claims about the effects of literature – or creative communications in Boykoff's terminology – literary education and literacy research have vital contributions to make. Per Esben Myren-Svelstad, literary scholar and educator, rightly speaks of 'a need for a more fundamental theoretical discussion of the relations between literature, literary ethics, and education for sustainability' (2020, 1). His notion of 'sustainable literary competence' provides useful and inspiring groundwork for some of the ideas we develop here, and we want to provide possible answers to his question: 'what are the pedagogically useful links between imaginative literature, literary competence, and ecological thinking?' (2). Without adding yet another highly specialised form of literacy to the wide array of literacies on offer, we hope that our notion of climate change literacy will help to readjust the understanding and usage of concepts of literacy in current anglophone educational systems considering the all-encompassing challenge of climate change and risks of extinction. Literacy, we argue, needs to be reclaimed by humanities disciplines that aren't content with the predominant, merely technical and linear understanding of skill-oriented intervention which, as Sasha Matthewman contends, 'really began to eat away at the power of English to develop pupils' values in relation to the world around them' (2011, 43). We therefore propose to rethink and promote climate change literacy as a key element of the environmental humanities, and structure the following argument into three parts.

Section 1 begins with observations on literacy and climate change communication. After briefly surveying conceptions of complex literacies in the sciences, we also draw on research in the field of so-called New Literacy Studies, where literacy is not so much understood as a compartmentalised skill but as a relation (Gee 2015). Such an understanding has much to offer for the relational practice of literary reading, which is, as Sofia Ahlberg notes, 'far from isolated activity. Rather, there is a vital connection between reading and living, reading and knowing the world, reading and discovering the world, as well as reading and intervening in the world' (2021, 13; see also Bartosch 2017). This relationality helps us tap into the full potential of aesthetic engagement with climate change – especially so since the 'diverse spatial and temporal scales of this "wicked problem" demand more of the humanities than the mere translation of climate science for lay readers' (Siperstein et al. 2017, 3). At the heart of the problem of many notions of (advanced) literacy, for example risk or health literacy, lies the 'mind-behaviour gap', the discrepancy between human knowledge and action, that is also such a familiar challenge in climate change communication. Probing this gap, we proceed to address two common fallacies in debates about how literature might 'work', namely the cognitive and the sentimental fallacies, concluding with the observation that neither a fixation on facts nor on emotions is sufficient. We then suggest rethinking climate change literacy as a particular form of thought or relation with the world – 'thinking twice' – enabled through literary reading that is both 'fast' and 'slow', with reference to psychologist Daniel Kahneman's (2012) distinction between different systems of thought.

Section 2 is concerned with interpretations of 'cli-fi' literature environments, a term we use to capture the interaction of narrative form and function.

We investigate this interaction by presenting and discussing elements of our select novels' structure and narrative composition, their ability to involve readers, as well as the texts' exploration of socio-ecological complexity. In lieu of cognitive and sentimental fallacies, we argue that climate change literacy requires attention to the ways in which literary narrative situates climate change within a larger cultural context and re-situates questions of reflexion and agency accordingly. We make the case by organising this understanding of climate change literacy around three interrelated concepts and demonstrate how they operate in and through the narratives: (1) discourse awareness (which includes ideas such framing, scaling, and foregrounding), (2) critical empathy (which focuses on perspective and identification), and (3) systems thinking (which includes intersectionality and matters of justice). Throughout the section, we work with established concepts from literary ecocriticism and narratology, while also drawing on theoretical and empirical work on the role of embodied cognition, readerly transportation, and identification (e.g., Martínez 2018; Weik von Mossner 2017a). The discussion reveals the literary-theoretical and educational distinctions between identificatory readings on the textual surface level and the more sustainable and pedagogically desirable forms of reception that align form and content. Jointly, the readings highlight the aspects that make up climate change literacy, but also show that literary reading ultimately requires mediation and certain literacy environments.

The latter are introduced in Section 3, concerned more explicitly still with the theory and practice of teaching climate fiction. To grasp the potential of literature in the educational debate on literacy, this part translates our findings from previous discussions into an educational concept that centres on interpretation and analysis, reflexion and readerly agency rather than emotional identification or scientific understanding. It brings home our earlier points that climate change literacy helps understand what is usually referred to as the mind-behaviour gap on the basis of the texts themselves. Moreover, we argue that its key characteristic is a novel understanding of the cultured phenomenon of climate and of socio-ecological complexities, and we identify methodological constraints and opportunities for the literature classroom. Suggesting to proceed on three levels that we call the '3Ts' (Texts, Textures, and Tasks), this section returns to the idea that literacy involves a synthesised form of thinking complexity as 'thinking twice' and relates it to the idea of critical reader agency (and what we discuss as acting-in-language, crucial for any form of meaningful climate action). The Afterword of this Element then moves the discussion of climate change literacy 'beyond cli-fi', opening avenues of further research, teaching, and reading.

1 Literacy and Climate Change Communication

Probing the Mind-Behaviour Gap

Our lives are influenced by the stories we tell and by how these stories are told. Stories are crucial for making sense and providing orientation – but it is less clear how exactly these processes play out in individuals and whether it is possible to formally design learning situations based on such highly individual processes. The concept of literacy helps to approach such questions, and it is through both literary and literacy research that we want to enter a conversation about the idea that fiction can complement and enrich climate change communication. Climate change communication is a broad interdisciplinary field of research of its own (see Holmes and Richardson 2020) and cannot be conflated with the kind of ecocritical and ecopedagogical work we are primarily concerned with. Yet, an important avenue for discussing shared concerns in both fields opens when considering the diagnosis that 'more information about climate change has not adequately addressed the chronic challenges of climate literacy, public awareness and engagement' (Boykoff 2019, 1). When Boykoff concludes that 'more creative approaches are needed to more effectively meet people where they are on climate change' (1), we suggest that literary and cultural research and pedagogy in the environmental humanities can provide valuable insights into the working of such creative communications – and to not only meet people where they are but to help them move further to explore hitherto uncharted imaginative territory.

To date, however, the dominant understanding of literacy when it comes to climate change is 'science literacy' or 'climate literacy'. Typically, these concepts are proposed as umbrella terms for the various competencies and skills needed to bridge a gap between understanding the sciences of climate change and acting on the grounds of this knowledge. The gap between the two – knowledge and appropriate behaviour – is a well-known psychological problem, variously labelled 'mind-', 'attitude-' or 'intention-behaviour gap', which, in fact, doesn't just apply to climate change (see Kollmus and Agyeman 2002; UNESCO 2017). The fact that knowing stuff does not necessarily imply a translation of this knowledge into action bugs researchers across the board. It is therefore not so surprising that, as Krista Hiser and Matthew Lynch explain in a recent study of climate literacy among college students in the US, 'concern does not always translate to action. There is a "know-do" gap that seems to keep an individual, group, or nation from moving attained knowledge into required action' (2021, 2; note the different terminologies in use – for reasons of clarity, we only use 'mind-behaviour gap' from now on). That such a gap exists is interesting; what seems equally notable is that literacy's original meaning of referring to fundamental skills of reading and writing has been modified and come to mean 'understanding science plus individual or collective action'. This equation, also familiar in related contexts such as health literacy, however, underrates the complexity of individual and collective cultural responses to what, as argued previously, is still often framed largely as a scientific problem.

Countless psychological studies on sustainability and on risk behaviour confirm that neither purely information-based nor primarily emotional communications alone can bridge the mind-behaviour gap. The divide between what people know and think and what they will act on, ultimately, is a tricky issue on a variety of counts. What makes it even more complex in the context of climate action is that the climate crisis is both urgent and endless. It therefore requires quick *and* thorough responses while also ruling out simple solutions and the short-term gratification of a successful resolution. In fact, inquiring how to bridge the mind-behaviour gap in the case of climate change might mean asking the wrong questions altogether. From the perspective of literary education, the focus on behavioural change is based on faulty assumptions about learning and sustainability – as might be the focus on climate as such. Paradoxically, Mike Hulme notes, '[j]ust as imagining the climatic future cannot be left to *science* alone, so imagining the future cannot be reduced to *climate* alone' (2021, 228). Consequently, our discussion of climate change literacy is situated within a heterogeneous discursive field that encompasses other literacies and research related to them, including, for instance, futures literacy and global learning.

By suggesting that one of the benefits of reading literary fiction lies in experiences of socio-ecological complexities, we respond to writer Margaret Atwood's (2015) insightful proposition that instead of climate change, we should rather refer to the current and future climatic predicament as 'everything change'. Yet, how can one conceive of a specific literacy – an acquired ability – that is about 'everything'? For one, the focus needs to shift from a specific form of construing climate change – namely, a merely technical, scientific, and solutionist understanding – to a recognition of the importance of engaging with complexity and connections between seemingly disparate issues that are both natural and cultural and undercut any clear-cut separation between these two realms. In addition, it is necessary to avoid any myopic focus on information or emotion alone and instead to cherish the complex enmeshment of readers and narrative in processes of climate reckoning. For reasons of practicality and the sake of our general argument, we are leaving aside important questions regarding the acquisition and support of basic literacy here. While the ability to read and write is, of course, prerequisite to our understanding of climate change literacy, addressing this would require a different book altogether. Furthermore, while arguments about a processual acquisition of relevant literacy, starting with basic environmental knowledge and culminating in critical response and action, have been made (for example by Stables 2006; Küchler 2017), we are hesitant to relegate critical literary understanding to the margins of advanced literacies, needed by all, but acquired by few.

We see meaningful connections between calls for greater climate change literacy and research on the challenges of literacy in other realms, such as in health (risk) literacy. During the past two years of the COVID-19 pandemic and struggling vaccination campaigns, this form of literacy has received even more public attention than before (see Hoydis 2021, 94). Here, too, literacy means a multidimensional understanding of both scientific fact and critical reflection as well as individual forms of agency and behaviour. The COVID-Health Literacy Network defines it as the advancing of understanding about health, of 'a critical tool to navigate information, sources and services', and the translation of 'knowledge into practical action' (COVID-HL Network 2021). In pre-COVID times, a team of researchers around Christina Zarcadoolas described health literacy similarly, if even more sweepingly, as 'the ability to understand scientific concepts, content, and health research; skills in spoken and written, and online communication; critical interpretation of mass media messages; navigating complex systems of health care and governance; and knowledge and use of community capital and resources, as well as using cultural and indigenous knowledge' (Zarcadoolas et al. 2006, 53). Immediately, one is struck by the complexity of such a definition of literacy, which arguably connects knowledge and understanding of facts with multimodal ways of communication as well as demands on critical evaluation and the integration of different, potentially incommensurate forms of knowledge. Meanwhile, the fact that the first step in accessing and processing the required information (usually print or digital texts) essentially means *reading* and *understanding narratives* is, for obvious reasons, rarely mentioned.

One encounters an equally broad mix in established concepts of climate or science literacy, which all seek to connect knowledge of facts and appropriate attitudes and behaviours, hinging on fuzzy notions of 'action', as a brief review of studies and materials shows: The US Global Research Program 2009, *Climate Literacy: The Essential Principles of Climate Science*, for instance, defines climate literacy as an 'understanding [of] essential principles of Earth's climate system, assessment of scientific information; meaningful communication about climate change; making informed and responsible decisions with regard to actions that may affect climate' (2009, n.p). This conception occurs in many, only slightly varying formulations across websites of governmental science and educational agencies of the past decade. A similar link between comprehension and action underlies the notion of climate literacy, as formulated by Daniel Shepardson, Anita Rouchoudhury, and Andrew Hirsch, who commit to transforming 'students' conceptualisation of global warming and climate change, such that they become informed decision makers' (Shepardson et al. 2017, ix; see Hufnagel 2017, 43). A third suggestion, this time from the humanities and aimed at sustainability rather than climate as such, defines sustainability literacy as '[t]he ability to take steps towards building a more sustainable self and society' and is interested in nothing less than the 'skills, attitudes, competencies, dispositions and values that are necessary for surviving and thriving in the declining conditions of the world in ways which slow down that decline as far as possible' (Stibbe and Luna 2009, 10). The reliance of these (and other) literacy concepts on individual agency and the ability to change or 'transform' simultaneously self, society, and climate is remarkable (see also Schneidewind 2013). To us, it seems a tall order indeed for individual learners, and one that potentially occludes the political dimension of an ecological transformation that calls for stronger stuff than sustainable consumer decisions (see Stengers 2015, 31; Ideland 2019; Bartosch 2020). Most importantly, by linking a fact-based understanding of climate and the normative dimensions of appropriate response and action, these suggestions painfully ignore the role and potential of imaginative thought as a key component of (climate change) literacy. Current psychological research on perception and decision-making (Klöckner 2020) indicates that the imagination does play a key role indeed – but this role might be different than the one assigned by science- and action-oriented intervention research.

Before turning to the role of literary reading, a brief note on a conception of agency is in order that is useful to develop the fuzzy notions of responsible action in debates of climate (science) literacy. Also writing about scientific literacy, Karen Barad notes how this concept is called upon for a great number of rationales, including the promotion of rational thinking, individual decision-making, *and* democracy, or as a condition for cultural literacy. And yet, what exactly being 'literate' in all these contexts means beyond 'knowing facts' is unclear (Barad 2000, 225). She also cautions that, even though it 'is called upon to perform a host of vital tasks concerning the future well-being of the nation and its individuals, by any of the standard measures, it remains an illusive goal' (225). Clearly, the same goes for most conceptions of literacy in relation to climate change. While Barad's argument, based on her own teaching experience, reiterates that the successful transmission of (factual) knowledge remains a challenge, it also promotes a framework for what should follow from it: responsible action in the real world. In her understanding, this 'intra-action', which she terms '*agential realism*', is made up of both material and discursive phenomena and includes learning how to analyse, imagine, and understand practices and possibilities (235; 237). This is part and parcel of the engagement with literary fiction. In this sense, climate change literacy does entail but also transcends knowledge of facts about climate change and methods of literary and cultural analysis. This ability of 'knowing how to intra-act responsibly within the world' – rather than taking specific action like, let's say, recycling after reading a novel about waste and finite resources – might go some length in circumventing the mind-behaviour gap, redefining what counts as responsible *action*. It might help to prepare 'future generations to meet the challenges that lie ahead' (246), although this endeavour must inevitably cut across curricula and disciplines.

Thus far we have observed how approaches to climate literacy ignore the potential of the humanities, literary studies and literature pedagogy in particular, although, strangely enough, research on literacy is part of the disciplinary DNA of these fields. We therefore want to reclaim some authority on the notion of literacy and complement conversations on literacy in the context of climate change and are convinced that such a move is both rewarding and necessary. A more diverse notion of climate change literacy speaks to demands in climate communication research for more creative forms of communication and engagement. It also underlines the importance of empowering readers to other, arguably more pro-ductive forms of reception: based on literary and aesthetic experience, an aware-ness of narrative complexity and the affordances different media – novels, but also short stories, plays, poetry, films, and video games – have to offer.

That information and emotional engagement have so far dominated the debate of what climate fiction can 'do' is hardly surprising if one sees in this preoccupation an echo of the age-old notion that literature and narrative's main concern is to be useful and to entertain: the Horatian formula *prodesse et delectare* has featured prominently in historical debates on the role and function of fiction, in Europe and elsewhere (see, e.g., Grabes 2008; Kössinger and Wittig 2019). It now makes a forceful new entry through debates on the usefulness and entertainment value of fiction in the context of climate action. It doesn't suffice, however, to emphasise the advantage of more entertaining forms of communication or informative fictions at the expense of more complex concerns with aesthetic reception and experience. We address such simplistic attempts of conceptualising literacy by identifying two fallacies that we term the cognitive and the sentimental fallacy. (The latter term might evoke the New Criticism's concept of the affective fallacy – from which we will ultimately move away, as will be clear herein.) We substantiate our claims about the influence of these two fallacies with references to communication and reception studies from a variety of fields, including psychology, film studies, and empirical or cognitive ecocriticism.

Returning to what was said at the beginning of this section, we are re-adjusting the argument about literary fiction and its powerful grasp, because the debate about whether or not behaviour can be modified by means of knowledge and understanding concerns literature education and climate change communication alike. And in both fields, it is far from settled. In an insightful review of research on the mind-behaviour gap, Anja Kollmus and Julian Agyeman write: 'Numerous theoretical frameworks have been developed to explain the gap between the possession of environmental knowledge and environmental awareness, and displaying pro-environmental behavior. Although many hundreds of studies have been done, no definitive answers have been found' (2002, 240). This humbling assessment notwithstanding, literary theorists and educators entertain an unwavering hope in the ethics of reading and that reading fiction might, in some way or other, lead to more sustainable behaviour, to responsible decision-making, and 'better' attitudes. Myren-Svelstad identifies an 'altruistic paradigm of ecocritical pedagogy' underlying this hope and criticises this assumption about behavioural functions and literature for several reasons. Not only is it far from certain how the transfer from knowledge to action can be modelled on literary writing; more importantly, such a functional understanding is selling short fiction's capacity to deal with complexity and uncertainty. Indeed, one might argue that its main function is to foster ambiguities rather than actions. On these grounds, Myren-Svelstad points out that 'using imaginative literature as a way of relaying information on the environment seems to rest on an "information deficit model" of environmental action' and concludes: 'even if readers did develop knowledge of, and caring attitudes towards, the environment by reading literature, it is not obvious that this would lead to more sustainable practices in the real world' (2020, 3).

So, what do readers stand to gain by engaging with climate fiction? Like Myren-Svelstad, we seek to promote the potential of literature in educational contexts by focusing on questions of complexity and ambiguity to make a better case for the importance of literacy in climate and environmental education. This requires rethinking what literature can and what it shouldn't be expected to do. As Garrard recounts in a reflection of his own experiences of teaching novels and short stories to sustainability students, 'I tried to dissuade the students from seeing the selected climate fiction as evidence for or against any of these explanations [of climate change], but rather as *dramatizations* of the cultural processes by which climate change becomes cognitively and emotionally legible' (2017, 122). His conviction that 'narrative technique functions as a *cognitive technology* that shapes our comprehension of climate change' (122) suggests a more nuanced understanding of the working of literature beyond simple cause-and-effect schemas. Arguing along the same lines,

Alexandra Nikoleris, Johannes Stripple, and Paul Tenngart underline specific-ally the function of climate fiction to explore complex scenarios as 'learning machines', 'not "truth machines"' (Nikoleris et al. 2017, 308).

It is therefore important to be wary of master narratives about the ethical or behavioural effects of reading that do justice neither to individual and diverse reading responses nor to the complexity of meaning as it evolves. Facile claims about the ethical value of fiction, Myren-Svelstad reminds us, might reflect a desire 'to justify literary studies by their supposed ethical effects' (2020, 3). While it seemingly offers a relatively easy way for literary scholarship and education to safeguard the relevance of allegedly 'soft' skills such as reading and hermeneutic interpretation, and to claim their value vis-à-vis the hard sci-ences, it partially misses the complexities – and therefore the unique potential – of literature and the 'unpredictability in reactions of readers' (3–4). Consequently, what follows is not another defence of literary studies but a suggestion how to better deal with the myriad ways in which literature engages with climate and other complexities – after probing a little deeper why putting all bets on cognition and emotion might be a bad idea.

The Cognitive Fallacy: Why Facts Aren't Enough

In theory, it's simple enough: There is a looming catastrophe; there are facts to prove it. Still people don't act as they should to avoid catastrophe – although they could, and there's data and facts to rely on in the process. This, as we have seen, sums up the conundrum of the mind-behaviour gap. What follows, then, is that either the facts aren't clear, or that they need to be communicated better: the latter option brings us back to the struggle of communicating climate change or any other enduring crisis, such as the global COVID-19 pandemic. If people only *knew* and *understood* their house was on fire, wouldn't they start running or fetching buckets of water or at least phone someone to help fight it? This has been the logic behind what is known as the information-deficit model of climate change communication (Boykoff 2019, 54–64). Information must be transmit-ted, and if the desired effects fail to materialise, it must be transmitted more effectively. After all, as a much-loved myth insists, humans are rational crea-tures and act upon knowledge and conviction – or so many still like to believe.

The so-called gateway-belief model from psychological and communicative research contains one of the most powerful articulations of such hopes concern-ing rational choices (van der Linden et al. 2017). Linking poor choices with deficits in knowledge suggests more knowledge as the logical way to arrive at better choices. However, as has been demonstrated time and again by crisis and risk experts struggling to convey complex (climate) knowledge to the general public, if the knowledge cannot be processed and applied, the remaining option is to have faith that people will still trust it. The hope that people will trust and understand *eventually* is why scientists should not tire informing the public about scientific consensus on the issue of climate change – a consensus, which is, in fact, impressive (see Oreskes 2004). Still, it appears to not quite do the trick. The hope behind the gateway-belief model is that consensus messaging and the perceived scientific consensus will increase individual worries about climate change, rendering support of public action the only logical outcome.

Research has shown that repeated exposure to consensus messaging is indeed conducive to greater levels of support (van der Linden et al. 2017). Yet this effect occurs only if people trust science in the first place. It moreover simplifies the concerns over climate change by way of turning it into a matter of science only, something we are arguing against throughout this Element. In addition, such an understanding of scientific consensus cannot do justice to the complexities of climate change denial and inaction, as one of the much rarer studies of climate change scepticism points out (Garrard et al. 2019). And, as a group of researchers around sociologist Warren Pearce have maintained, the notion of producing proof by way of consensus messaging overlooks important aspects – of ideology and value as much as of the normative dimensions of global policy challenges: 'Climate science is complex and findings often contradictory and, most importantly, do not tell us anything about what to do about climate change' (Pearce et al. 2017, 725). This means that even if consensus leads to worry about and belief in anthropogenic climate change, support for public action can only work either in a very abstract or specific sense. In an abstract sense, it means an awareness of urgency and relevance – without direct implications for right forms of action. The specific sense includes measures of dealing with a local effect of climate change. Yet the fact remains that science can only show that current and future levels of greenhouse gases in the atmosphere have dangerous effects, and it cannot offer solutions in the sense of whether it is best to go solar, nuclear, or something else entirely, whether one should become vegan, stop having children, or simply wait to see what happens. In other words, the *cognition* of climate change doesn't translate easily into a *rational* or *normative* response. Instead, it might produce cognitive dissonance, especially if people notice that their immediate surroundings or the world at large do not support and even counteract any attempt to act responsibly on what they know. This whole debate also cannot ignore that, while there is consensus about scientific facts, the question what constitutes a rational response or responsible behaviour will produce very different answers depending on peoples' location on this planet.

Polls and other forms of research in educational contexts on the impact of information on student behaviour have also underlined that such translation from knowledge to action is indeed difficult (see Hall 2015, 2–3; as well as studies on the 'Enlightenment myth' of rational choice and forms of denial by Norgaard (2011); Cohen (2001); and Lakoff (2004)). Matters only get worse once literary fiction enters the stage: what, if any, facts can be deduced from reading novels, and what do we do with such facts once we know that they don't necessarily benefit processes of rational choice? Despite these far-reaching questions, 'knowledge' remains a principal concern in concepts of climate or sustainability literacies and related competences, as does the assumption that knowledge (often sold as 'awareness') will eventually result in 'action' – this is precisely what we call the cognitive fallacy.

The Sentimental Fallacy: Why Emotions Aren't Enough

The preceding discussion doesn't call into question that stories include facts or that storytelling helps memorise and make sense of facts. But if literature's status as intricate make-believe is taken seriously, great care is warranted when talking about the learning of facts from fiction. It thus might be a safer bet to focus on fiction's ability to move us. Art and aesthetic experience have a lot to do with affect, and undoubtedly art's capacity to move people plays a large part in drawing audiences to it. So, as with the cognitive fallacy, our point of contention with the sentimental fallacy is one of simplistic reasoning. While idealist educators continue to proclaim that reading literature makes us more empathetic and emotionally mature human beings, it is much harder to say how this process works, let alone how it might be tested and designed in educational processes. As Milkoreit concludes, such aspirations are often 'fuelled by hope rather than observation' (2016, 177). This doesn't contradict research, especially in affective ecocriticism and cognitive literary studies, that offers tools to explore in depth the emotionalising strategies of specific environmental narratives (see Weik von Mossner 2017a). It rather calls into question the idea that such strategies necessarily bring about the desired emotional, attitudinal, and behavioural effects.

What is more, the discussion around fiction and climate action began by largely building on an idea that has proved equally difficult to sustain: that mostly terrible and terrifying stories, inciting negative and fearful emotions, might lead to better and more sustainable behaviours by shocking people into action. This is an awful idea especially when it comes to young learners and prospective readers. It also rests on the flawed assumption that emotional response can be used in this way at all. As any behavioural psychologist can tell us, powerful and overwhelming emotion does not have to lead to 'productive' action. Accordingly, the next bet, especially in the environmental humanities and within climate change communication, was therefore on inspiring optimism and hope, rather than fear (Mauch 2019). This is driven by 'a mounting body of literature' indicating, as Matthew Cole explains, 'that attempts to marshal urgency through fear lead to denial, disillusionment, and apathy rather than action' (2022, 136). But this doesn't imply that more optimistic scenarios work any better.

The problem we see is that both approaches (seeking to inspire fear or hope) share the underlying assumption that powerful emotional storytelling can make readers more climate literate by moving them to action. Implicitly, scholars and educators thus tend to conceive of emotions as a switch that can be turned on or off for a specific effect. Be it in the positive sense (when stories provide role models or model successful forms of climate action and sustainability transitions) and in the negative (when gloom-and-doom apocalypses are expected to change our ways because cautionary tales help us to understand the reasons for decline and demise). Only things aren't that simple, once again. As Daniel Chapman, Brian Lickel, and Ezra Markowitz explain, '[t]he bifurcation between "go positive" and "go negative" simultaneously oversimplifies the rich base of research on emotion while overcomplicating the very real communications challenge advocates face by demanding that each message have the right "emotional recipe" to maximize effectiveness' (2017, 852). One might try and insert 'teachers' here for 'advocates', and accept that switches and recipes don't exist when it comes to teaching literature either.

Still, it appears tempting, and common-sense really, to focus on 'heartfelt stories of personal motivations to active engagement', as Boykoff (2019, 145) writes. Empirical research might give us pause though: heartfelt stories do not necessarily sustain engagement and values but have only short-term effects. As Schneider-Mayerson and his colleagues in the empirical ecocriticism project have shown (see Schneider-Mayerson et al. 2020), issues of empathy and emotional engagement might even produce the opposite effect. Taking readerly responses to the depiction of climate refugees in Paolo Bacigalupi's SF novel *The Water Knife* as his example, he notes in an interview with Amy Brady: 'Authors and critics might hope that portraying a dystopic cautionary future will scare readers into engaging in progressive politics today, but it might not work out that way. A vivid depiction of desperate climate migrants engaged in a self-interested and violent struggle for survival can backfire, since even liberal readers might not empathize with climate migrants, but fear them' (2020, n.p).

Current empirical research on readerly reception is helpful not only because it challenges facile notions of behavioural change based on literary experience. It also calls for the development of better understandings of key concepts by which we identify such reaction in the first place. For example, it makes sense to assume that identification with characters – via eco-heroines or other role models – will trigger sympathetic reader responses and lead to more courageous or altruistic behaviour. And yet we need to diversify conceptions of 'identification' if we want to understand why fictional characters cannot model and influence human behaviour in any linear and superficial way.

This is not a novel idea. Writing about a branch of literature known for centuries for inciting strong affect in readers, horror fiction, Noël Carroll provides insights into the complex relationship between character and reader. He identifies 'paradoxical' ways of reception and identification in horror literature, taking stock of audience reaction to monstrous beings 'whose ontological status is that of thought contents' – and that are unlikely to be role models or bearers of sympathy. He concludes that while identification 'is a common notion in everyday talk about fiction', research should better understand the metaphorical dimension of the idea of identification with fictional characters, which 'could mean a range of things and could be connected to a variety of different psychological theories' (1990, 89). Current cognitive and empirical research offers helpful additions and evidence for the complexity of relations that Carroll calls 'character-identification' and that includes the options

> that we like the protagonist; that we recognize the circumstances of the protagonist to be significantly like those we have found or find ourselves in; that we sympathize with the protagonist; that we are one in interest, or feeling, or principle, or all of these with the protagonist; that we see the action unfolding in the fiction from the protagonist's point of view; that we share the protagonist's values; that, for the duration of our intercourse with the fiction, we are entranced (or otherwise manipulated and/or deceived) so that we fall under the illusion that each of us somehow regards herself to be the protagonist. (89)

We are therefore called to carefully rethink the idea of identification and emotional engagement if we want to reconcile close readings of select texts with a more appropriate sense of what readings will and can do in processes of readerly reception. Only then are we able to situate emotional connections with fiction within climate change literacy.

Rethinking Climate Change Literacy

Having understood better what questions we *shouldn't* ask, we can now turn to what climate change literacy can do when it is based on literary fiction. For this, we must avoid being reductionist: In his critical assessment of recent attempts to use storytelling and aesthetics more generally to better communicate climate science, Hulme challenges their prevalent assumption that art can and should be 'appropriated as a handmaiden to science' (2021, 152). Instead, he avers, 'creative engagement with the idea of climate change is about using different cultural media to disrupt taken-for-granted representations of climate change. It is about "thickening" people's understanding of climate change rather than disciplining it' (155).

Now, how can literature help in 'thickening' understanding? One important cue comes from Hulme's endorsement of ecocritical methods, as he writes that '[t]hrough a close-reading of texts, ecocriticism is more likely to expose ambivalences about what climate change *is*, people's anxieties about the future, and the nature of the predicament climate change presents us with' (2021, 157). It seems that close-reading literary texts can help to grasp climate change beyond scientific facts yet without disregarding them – and this is because of the readiness of literature to thrive on, rather than reduce, ambiguity. 'Literature', Hulme sums up,

> has a unique ability to capture the complexity and ambiguity of everyday human experience. Through the medium of story-telling, novels are able to negotiate between competing cultural values and convey contrary experiences of class, race, and gender. They are able to provoke reflection about our actions in the world in relation to the subjectivities of others and the imagined possibilities of an unknown future. (158)

This is an important first lesson for climate change literacy research in the environmental humanities: focus on ambiguity and complexity. This focus might support us in re-imagining what 'awareness' may mean beyond mere technical knowledge of facts and might point to ways of grasping socio-ecological rather than climate-scientific complexities.

The second lesson pertains to the fact that the forms of 'slow' reading that characterise literary interpretations do not satisfy those who seek immediate and decisive climate action as the key to sustainability transformations. Especially when it comes to issues of behaviour and behavioural change, research on the speed and effect of aesthetic response is a complex matter – but nonetheless exciting and encouraging: it has shown that contact with works of art can be 'powerful enough to be the starting point of a person's journey through behavioural change' (Klöckner 2020, 121). And yet, to ascertain this is very different from assuming that reading will kick off major behavioural change. It is rather a trigger and a means of inciting transformation by powerfully reframing ways of seeing and thinking – thickening perception is quite unlike suggesting we should change our diet or recycle more thoroughly. Psychologist Christian Klöckner explains this by referring to 'a behaviour change model from the health domain' (119) that distinguishes *predecision* (i.e., understanding why action is necessary), *pre-action* (which action to choose), *action*, and *post-action*. If we follow this terminology, literature has only a little role to play in action and post-action phases but makes a crucial difference in predecision phases. It is here that it can incite moments of recognition and understanding in the first place and regarding issues that would otherwise not be identified at all or with less complexity. As Klöckner concludes, 'being confronted with the artwork alone seems to be not enough to progress through the *whole* process of change' (121) – but it can be central to initiating moments of transformative thought that are no less relevant because they engender, rather than translate into, considerations about action, value, and thought.

It is important to note that Klöckner goes on to argue that political participation, rather than the incessantly demanded behavioural change, is 'perhaps the most important behaviour people can enact in democratic societies' (117). This points to the fact that individual mind-behaviour gaps are not as crucial as the ability and willingness to engage in collaboration and communication about climate. The educational concept of *Sprachhandeln* (translatable as action-in-language) lends itself to this context and shifts attention from individual behaviour change towards communicative forms of climate action. Even if we agree that literature can 'only' help with the first, predecision stage and is thus deficient in a certain sense, we can argue that this first stage is much more difficult to attain than later ones, which can do with constant messaging, social marketing, and related forms of nudging – and, indeed, direct political action. This is not the prerogative of literature or literature pedagogy, however. Bringing about transformative perception and instilling meaningful communication *is*.

Such flashes of transformative thinking in predecision phases, however, have little to do with the notion of slow thinking. But do we have to decide for a speed limit? It makes sense to consider another ambiguity of the literary, having to do with perception, cognition, affect – and different ways of processing information and emotion. We doubt that these two forms of processing can be neatly distinguished at all. Work by Antonio Damasio and Vittorio Gallese and others on embodied cognition and the rationality of feelings suggests that understanding, and aesthetic understanding in particular, cannot be explained by way of any facile dichotomy between rational cognition and affective or emotional response. Rather, both forms of engaging with the world are in constant conversation. Overemphasising one at the expense of the other comes at the risk of missing out on the complexity of thinking, or what Brian Massumi calls 'the thinking-feeling of what happens' (2008). To us, 'thinking-feeling' sounds a lot like what is going on when we read fiction – which brings us back to the question of 'slow' or any other speed of processing.

The distinction between 'thinking fast and slow' was famously introduced by economic psychologist and Nobel Laureate Daniel Kahnemann. We are convinced that it helps to better grasp what happens when we read – and learn through – fiction, and how literacy designs may support such processes. In his popular 2011 book, Kahnemann references a well-established distinction in psychological research between two systems of thinking, or, as he calls it, between thinking 'fast' and 'slow': '*System 1* operates automatically and quickly, with little or no effort and no sense of voluntary control' whereas '*System 2* allocates attention to the effortful mental activities that demand it' (2012: 20–1). For our purposes, this distinction is as important as Kahnemann's observation that '[t]he operations of System 2 are often associated with the subjective experience of agency, choice, and concentration' (21). Beginning with the distinction itself, we must ask ourselves what it means for literary reading – does it require and foster a fast or a slow form of thinking? Arguably, aesthetic perception is one, if not the, primary example of fast thinking that happens 'automatically and quickly' – for instance when we perceive a mood or atmosphere, or when we are struck by beauty or relate to artworks in any of the numerous ways that Rita Felski (2008, 2020) has explored and systematised so succinctly. But as Noël Carroll noted in 1990 already, what is crucial when being affected in the reception of literature is the 'willing suspension of disbe-lief' (in Coleridge's famous phrase): 'The victim of an illusion has had some-thing done to her; she has been caught unawares [. . .]. But the idea of a "*willing* suspension of disbelief" has an active air about it' (1990, 65). Is it thus rather an 'effortful mental activity' – an instance of the second system of thinking? While Carroll maintains that the notion of 'willing suspension' of beliefs makes little sense to him, it might be rewarding for literary educators to pay attention to the idea of two modes of thinking to identify the element of activity or agency that comes with the interpretive and necessarily slow forms of processing aesthetic experience. Kahnemann identifies this latter, slow form of thinking with 'agency, choice, and concentration'. Teachers know that these are part and parcel of literary learning, which challenges assumptions, often made by inex-perienced readers, that textual meaning is 'just there', on the page. At the same time, we know that aesthetic experience nonetheless happens to us, fast and full of complexity.

It thus seems that reading necessitates a curious mix of both systems of thought – in other words, it requires a form of 'thinking twice'. The reason why this is a helpful insight can be found in the description of both 'systems' that Kahnemann provides: the 'conscious, reasoning' self that governs System 2 is believed to be the one that 'makes choices, and decides what to think and what to do' (21). It is with System 1, however, that 'impressions and feelings' emerge that 'are the main source of beliefs and deliberate choices' (21). Notably, it is also where 'surprisingly complex patterns of ideas' are being generated,

although the 'orderly series of steps' created in System 2 remain relevant for
critical and complex thought operations. Taken together, this updates the
Romantic idea of a combination of powerful feelings and their recollection
(and possible revision) in tranquillity and, in our view, makes up the experience
of reading and interpretation. It also echoes and develops further the ideas of
late twentieth-century ethical criticism and research into the effects and teaching of literature by scholars such as Louise Rosenblatt (1978) and W.C. Booth
(1990). Their distinction between aesthetic and efferent reading puts similar
emphasis on two kinds of reading experience marked by different temporalities.
The first is aesthetic, instantaneous and less 'conscious', the second still influenced by the first, but 'efferent', reflective, and geared towards action. As Booth
puts it, efferent reading is motivated by 'the search either for some practical
guidance, or for some special wisdom, or for some other useful "carry-over"
into non-fictional life' (see 1990, 13; 14). Combining aesthetic affect and
derivative thought, the main concerns and constituents of climate change literacy can be addressed through this notion of 'thinking twice', as an equally fast
and slow form of thinking.

While one generally needs humility about all claims about how language and
perception work (see Maggs and Robinson 2020, 19), literary reading, as we
have been arguing thus far, can penetrate the mind's defences against climate
change by 'slowing us down' in the sense of helping to activate 'a more
expansive form of attention in our minds', as Hiser and Lynch (2021, 3) explain.
Literature negotiates sensory and emotional worlds; it invites critical reflection
as well as processes of empathy. Its effect, however, results from complex,
emergent processes of both fast and slow thinking, or 'thinking twice', as we put
it. This is crucial for its potential for climate change literacy: as our discussion
of the two fallacies indicates, neither a focus on pure fact nor unreflective
emotion is sufficient when it comes to the challenge of thinking about climate
change and acting upon this thinking. Moreover, a literary and aesthetic
response must entail understandings of complexity and what the scholar of an
ecology of mind, Gregory Bateson, describes as 'patterns that connect'
(Bateson 1972/2000; see also Kagan 2011; Zapf 2016). Then, instead of simple
linearity, patterns and connections of complexity emerge. Literature can go
a long way in a variety of things – but this does not mean that its best use is in
communicating science facts or bringing about behaviour change through
emotional manipulation. Rather, this emergence coincides, and depends upon,
'fast' forms of aesthetic experience in tandem with slower forms of interpretation and reflexion. Therefore, it is through thinking (at least) twice while
reading, through the equally fast and slow forms of literary experience that
the perception of climate complexity is sharpened – or 'thickened', in Hulme's

phrase. In Kahnemann's distinction, cognitive and sentimental fallacies place ill-advised emphasis on either System 1 or 2. A synthesis of both is what concerns us with climate change literacy – and it is from there that we move on to spelling out readerly interactions with literary texts in what we call 'literature environments'. For it certainly matters what 'company we keep', in Booth's (1990) memorable phrase, when it comes to the novels we read and the characters and story patterns we engage with, in addition to the topics that are foregrounded in the plot.

2 Cli-Fi Literature Environments

Much debate about how climate fiction works, we have argued in the previous section, is plagued by what we are calling the cognitive and sentimental fallacies. Acknowledging these fallacies implies two things: Fictional texts neither afford a straightforward, predictable transmission of facts. Nor do they trigger affects that then lead to responsible action in readers. It also indicates why literature isn't better suited per se to bridge the mind-behaviour gap than other kinds of texts or forms of climate change communication. But this does not mean that we no longer believe that the study of fictional texts has a lot to offer. This section sets out to elaborate what this might be, exactly, and uses narratological concepts to make its point. Whether the phenomenon of climate change (or the powerful yet evasive notion of the Anthropocene) resists narrativisation altogether or requires new and different kinds of storytelling continues to be a central question across the environmental humanities. This renders it even more striking, as Erin James observes, 'how absent the voices of narrative theorists are in this conversation'. She argues that 'the environmental humanities [...] would benefit from a stronger engagement with the lexicon and insights of narrative theory' (2022, 13; see also Gurr 2010). James's insightful work at the intersection of environmental and literary scholarship already goes a long way towards such an engagement. Helping to counteract the preference given to content over form – a persisting trend in cli-fi criticism and the environmental humanities (see 16) – James's *Narrative in the Anthropocene* (2022) seems, in fact, indicative of a wider recent shift towards form, demonstrated by other studies published around the same time, such as Marco Caracciolo's *Contemporary Fiction and Climate Uncertainty* (2022).

We seek to continue this conversation about literary form and, therefore, 'the work that readers must do to comprehend narratives, and the work that narratives do in terms of shifting the real-world attitudes, values, and behaviours of those readers, thus shaping the world in which we read' (James 2022, 14). And we seek to add another largely absent voice to it, that of literature pedagogy.

Econarratological studies such as the ones mentioned above typically neglect engagement with the question how findings from the analysis of texts and from narrative theory connect to teaching literature and fostering literacy (beyond notions of climate *science* literacy, as discussed in Section 1). These are precisely the questions that determine our selection of concepts in this section, which is concerned with *literature environments*. By this term we mean the texts and the interaction of narrative form and function, as well as the potential interaction between storyworlds and the real-life world of readers they enable.

The narratological concepts we identify in the following as crucial components of *discourse awareness* and *critical empathy* can of course be applied to reading all kinds of texts. But popular climate fiction exemplifies an understanding of narrative as 'worldbuilding for some purpose' (James 2022, 36) that is central here. Following James, we understand 'cli-fi' as a selection of texts that signal, or are widely perceived as doing so, 'an intention to prompt readers to think about and perhaps even reassess their understanding of anthropogenic climate change' (37). This draws attention to the fact that insights from rhetorical narrative theory implicitly underlie debates of climate fictions as persuasive tools of communication – 'for some purpose'. In addition, we also find it helpful to draw on cognitive narrative theory, as James does in her general definition of narrative in the Anthropocene, which combines approaches from both branches of narratology. In this conception, a narrative is '*somebody telling someone else on some occasion and for some purpose(s) that something happened in some world*' (28). This should indeed be kept in mind when asking what specific tools and strategies a text employs to guide readers – especially if these are learners and students – through storyworlds and how they relate to behavioural norms and values outside of them.

Both literary ecocriticism and narratology offer a rich conceptual toolkit for us. Amongst other things, they help to underline that while plot, the main events and their sequencing in the texts, are important, other hallmarks of narrativity such as temporality, spatialisation, and perspective (types of narrators and focalisation) are crucial, too, when it comes to addressing the cognitive and emotional effects and the two fallacies. As we have argued from the beginning, we share with ecocritics such as James or Garrard the strong disbelief in the existence of 'a golden ticket narrative', and doubt that the purpose of reading cli-fi is to eventually 'unearth the "perfect" story to shift public opinion and spur action toward a more responsible way of living in the world' (James 2022, 25). We are also acutely aware that reading preferences vary, and that degrees of literacy as well as numerous other sociocultural factors determine the reception of texts. Therefore, the corpus of texts we draw on for illustration is derived pragmatically from a survey of extant empirical and other critical studies of popular climate fiction (see Schneider-Mayerson 2018; Nikoleris et al. 2017, as well as Cole 2022, 138; Death 2022, 445). It includes T.C. Boyle's *A Friend of the Earth* (2000), Kim Stanley Robinson's *Forty Signs of Rain* (2004), Paolo Bacigalupi's *The Windup Girl* (2009), Ian McEwan's *Solar* (2010), Barbara Kingsolver's *Flight Behavior* (2012), Nathaniel Rich's *Odds Against Tomorrow* (2013), and, as an example of young adult fiction discussed in Section 3, Saci Lloyd's *The Carbon Diaries 2015* (2008).

These novels are exemplary in their popularity in the sense that their 'visibility and accessibility have been generally very high' (Nikoleris et al. 2017, 309). They have also generated a steadily growing body of scholarship as well as countless print and online reviews, as Schneider-Mayerson shows in his 2018 study, which considers entries on online review sites such as goodreads.com as a measure of popularity. Ranging from realist fiction to science fiction, the novels are all characterised by a more or less 'explicit focus on climate change [or environmental degradation generally] and their affirmation that it constitutes a grave threat to human societies and nonhuman life, in the present as well as the future' (Schneider-Mayerson 2018, 482). Each of these texts also has an entry in Goodbody and Johns-Putra's 2019 *CliFi: A Companion*. What we want to add to the discussion is a focus on their capacity to engender discourse awareness, critical empathy, and novel understandings of socio-ecological complexity, all of which are substantial components of climate change literacy. We begin by discussing discourse awareness as one fruitful response to the cognitive fallacy.

More than Facts: Enter Discourse Awareness

In the study of narrative, perhaps the most basic but also the most crucial distinction is the one between plot or story, and discourse. The first refers to a narrative's chronology of events and the (factual) topics addressed in it ('what happens'). The latter refers to the question 'how it is told' – the presentation and shaping of the narrative through language, rhetorical devices, and narrative strategies. Both levels are, of course, inseparably intertwined. But detaching plot from the discursive set-up remains an invaluable strategy for the analysis and interpretation of texts. The narratological understanding of discourse also resonates with concepts of discourse awareness in other related fields, especially language and literature education, where it is taken to refer primarily to an awareness of linguistic and stylistic phenomena, register and suchlike. Notably, it also resonates with research on the cultural engagement with climate, where climate change is itself best understood as a *discursive* phenomenon that is negotiated in different arenas and through different imaginaries as 'shared sets of beliefs, narratives, technologies, discourses and practices that condition what climate futures are thought of as possible, likely, or undesirable' (Hulme 2021, 230). In Hulme's *Why We Disagree about Climate Change*, the narrative construction of climate change is portrayed 'as a battleground' (2010, xxvii), utilised variably as justification, inspiration, or threat. Hulme also points to the narrative and, eventually, epistemological and political implications of each story template – the latter being of course a central object of study in narratology. To grasp these templates or patterns, to become aware of the discursive presentation of a complex scientific and cultural phenomenon such as climate change in a text, three concepts – framing, scaling, and foregrounding – are especially helpful.

Let's begin with *framing*. In sociology and social psychology, the concept of frames is used to explicate the organisation of experience. Frames contextualise, shape expectations and determine to large degrees what can be said and how statements are being read or understood. In literary narrative, framing pertains to how a story is told and contextualised, be it by abiding by rules of genre, through representational or rhetorical choices such as the use of humour or horror, the deliberate juxtaposition of events and perspectives and much more. Because framing plays such a crucial role in both fictional and nonfictional climate texts, climate change literacy needs an awareness of the strategic use of language and narrative conventions for desired effects, an understanding how the framing of certain episodes in a novel serves to highlight specific issues by representing events or developments in a certain light, or how and why scientific language differs from religious or techno-utopian frames. Since literary fictions confront us with multiple voices and viewpoints and can self-reflexively manipulate frames and reader expectations, we believe that climate change literacy has to start here.

A case in point is Ian McEwan's *Solar*. The novel's protagonist is London-based Nobel laureate scientist Michael Beard, a middle-aged man, struggling with a flagging career, health issues, and yet another failed marriage. Characterised by his self-centredness, denial of both personal and global problems, and inertia, he mainly seeks to maximise his own pleasure and personal gain. This leads him to steal research from a younger colleague, after being also complicit in his accidental death, which enables him to become involved in a solar energy scheme in New Mexico. Story and tone already challenge frame expectations in readers because neither the acidic humour nor a plotline of adultery, theft, and gluttony belongs to the standard repertoire of eco-hero story templates. But we find such deliberate takes on framing in individual scenes as well. Invited to give a long speech on climate science and mitigation strategies, Beard arrives late, gorges down nine greasy salmon sandwiches, and has to fight off nausea during his entire talk, which he opens by declaring: 'The planet [. . .]

is sick' (148). Reader's will either laugh or fight off disgust or nausea themselves, while the text establishes an underlying allegorical parallel between Beard's unhealthy physical condition and the planet. This scene culminates with Beard vomiting behind the curtain of the stage after his speech before joining the reception as if nothing happened (156). *Solar* ironically undermines the practice of factual 'info-dumping' – several pages full of details about climate science and the state of the planet given in the speech – by framing this with passages depicting the protagonist and main focaliser as a grotesquely undisciplined, erratic, and irresponsible character. Moreover, while this does not diminish the accuracy of his pronouncements, it does undermine ideas of straightforward transmission of factual knowledge through likeable and knowledgeable characters. The reader's task – as part of climate change literacy – is to recognise this framing through satire and allegory.

A similarly productive angle is provided by *scaling:* Climate change, as many scholars have noted, is a challenge to the imagination because it is 'at once wholly abstract and alarmingly material' (Garrard et al. 2014, 149) and names, as Hannes Bergthaller puts it, 'a process which takes place at scales vastly exceeding those of everyday experience, which is spatially and temporally diffuse, and whose reality can be grasped only by way of complex mathematical models incorporating knowledge from a wide array of scientific disciplines' (2018, v-2). It has therefore been argued that fiction might go a long way in providing 'sensuous representation of scales in space or time that greatly exceed immediate perception' (Clark 2019, 39), but climate remains a challenge to literary representation. As a plot event and topic, it is 'larger than usually makes for good fiction', as Bill McKibben (2011, 1) notes. And as motif, it might deflect from the fact that what is needed for a person to become more literate regarding the uneven effects of climate change is 'an intellectual practice attentive to the way the nature of an issue or situation alters according to the scale at which it is considered' (Clark 2019, 40).

This perception also underlies Timothy Morton's famous description of climate change as a 'hyperobject', by which he means 'things that are massively distributed in time and space relative to humans' (2013, 1). Hyperobjects cut across different scales, like the individual, national, and global or planetary, and becoming literate implies more than just scaling up (as in 'go global'). Rather, it necessitates an awareness of what Timothy Clark, using the metaphor of the 'carbon footprint', calls 'scale effects': 'The size of my carbon footprint is of no interest or significance except in relation to the incalculable effect of there being so many millions of other footprints having an impact on an uncertain timescale' (2015, 72). The narrativisation of climate change thus requires oscillation between the individual and the collective, the human and the nonhuman, the local and the global. This linking of, for example, individual life stories and the *grand narrative* of the whole planet is created through scaling. It is a form of 'imaginative zooming in and out' (Chakrabarty 2021, 137; see also James 2022, 159), and involves recognising, Clark explains, that taken together, seemingly insignificant individual actions have dramatic global consequences: 'for any individual household, motorist, etc. a scale effect in their actions is invisible', and 'progressive social and economic policies may [. . .] resemble, on another scale, an insane plan to destroy the biosphere' (2012, 150).

Temporal scaling in fiction sets short-term developments in the context of long-term, frequently imperceptible processes, often going back decades, centuries, millennia, or even millions of years, for instance in Kim Stanley Robinson's *Forty Signs of Rain,* the first volume in the SF trilogy 'Science in the Capital'. Set in the early twenty-first century, the novel highlights the effects of global warming, focusing mainly on a group of scientists, working in administration at the National Science Foundation in Washington D.C., or involved in biotech research or politics. They are later joined by a group of Buddhist monks working for the embassy and members of a fictional island nation, Khembalung, extremely threatened by rising sea levels. The narrative juxtaposes evolutionary and geological deep time with the daily routines of individual characters. This long-term perspective, it appears, is one of the functions of the ten short accounts – one to two pages each – of scientific backgrounds printed in italics before every major chapter:

> *At the end of the last Ice Age [. . .] vast shallow lakes were created by the melting of the polar ice cap. Eventually these lakes broke through their ice dams and poured off into the oceans. The Canadian shield still sports the scars from three or four of these cataclysmic floods [. . .]* Frank Vanderwaal kept track of climate news as a sort of morbid hobby. His friend Kenzo Hayakawa [worked] with the weather crowd on the ninth floor, and so Frank occasionally checked in with him to say hi and find out the latest. [The text continues with the trivia of work in the headquarters of the National Science Foundation.] (74; 75)

> *We are primates, very closely related to chimps and other great apes. Our ancestors speciated from the other apes about five million years ago, and evolved in parallel lines and overlapping subspecies, emerging most clearly as hominids about two million years ago. [. . .]* Anna was pleased to see Frank back in the office, brusque and grouchy though he was. (253; 255)

Pitting individual experiences and perspectives against collective and long-term consequences is of course what numerous (cli-fi) narratives do; as we will discuss below, *A Friend of the Earth* and *Flight Behaviour* generate their narrative dynamics from this very tension. Even narratives not primarily concerned with scale offer moments of experiencing scale effects that are important groundwork for larger considerations of understanding scale. Take the episode in which Beard descends onto London by plane:

> just below the trembling engine [. . .], his improbable destination, the micro-
> scopic airport, and around it, the arterial feeds, and traffic pulsing down them
> like corpuscles [. . .]. And now here it came again [. . .], the colossal disc of
> London itself, turning like an intricately spotted space station in majestic self-
> sufficiency. As unplanned as a giant termite nest, as a rain forest, and a thing
> of beauty. (McEwan 2010, 108)

Beard's eulogy on urban environments, and its bringing together a sublime sense of both the natural and the cultural, quickly turn into brooding and lamenting the threat of climate change:

> The giant concrete wounds dressed with steel [. . .] – the remains of the natural
> world could only shrink before them. The pressure of numbers, the abundance
> of inventions, the blind forces of desires and needs looked unstoppable and
> were generating a heat, a modern kind of heat [. . .]. The hot breath of civilisa-
> tion. He felt it, everyone was feeling it, on the neck, in the face. (109)

In this moment, Beard not so much grasps intellectually, but *senses* the scale of climate change, via the 'derangements of scale' (Clark) brought about by the mixing of nature, culture, the size of the city and his position and, later on, even the temporal scales of his childhood memories and the future. It is via Beard's perception that readers get in touch with the 'wholly abstract and alarmingly material' nature of climate change.

Scaling is a strategy of reducing but also maintaining complexity, as Bartosch (2019) has shown and, as Clark maintains, it 'usually enables a calibrated and useful extrapolation between dimensions of space and time. [. . .] With climate change, however, we have a map, its scale includes the whole earth but when it comes to relating the threat to daily questions of politics, ethics or specific interpretations of history, culture, literature, etc., the map is often almost mockingly useless' (2012, 148–9). This is exactly what *Solar* is doing: 'relating the threat to daily questions of politics, ethics or specific interpretations of history, culture, literature'. This also explains the suggestiveness of the 'boot room' scene: On an expedition to the Arctic, a group of highly educated climate-conscious and, by common standards, responsible artists and academics fail to maintain order in the room used to store boots, clothing, and other expedition equipment: 'the disorder in the boot room was noticeable [. . .] He suspected that he never wore the same boots on consecutive days. Even though he wrapped his goggles [. . .] in his inner balaclava on the third day, they were gone by the fourth, and the balaclava was on the floor, soaking up water' (73). The boot room episode negotiates the question of collective responsibility and individual egotism or carelessness. The text makes the connection to the global climate crisis and the challenge of scale explicit: 'How were they to save the earth – assuming it needed saving, which he doubted – when it was so much larger than the boot room' (109; see Hoydis 2019, 547; and Garrard 2013, 132).

Barbara Kingsolver's *Flight Behaviour* is equally attentive to scale, even to the point of turning scales into its basic narrative principle. The novel follows Dellarobia Turnbow, a young housewife and mother living on a sheep farm in present-day Appalachia in rural Tennessee. Discontented with her marriage and struggling to make ends meet, on a hill near her home she one day stumbles upon a beautiful sight she cannot comprehend: millions and millions of monarch butterflies. Soon, university professor Ovid Byron arrives to study the monarchs. He introduces Dellarobia, who becomes a sort of assistant to him, to a world of science and a thoroughly disturbing interpretation of the monarchs' gathering, as their flight patterns have been disrupted by climate change and they are likely to perish outside their regular habitat. Even the chapter headings make explicit the specific scales with which the events are connected. Taken together, they indicate in how far the novel engages in the act of 'zooming in and out' that was mentioned above as the foundation of understanding scale. Beginning with 'The Measure of a Man', subsequent chapters are titled 'Family Territory', 'Congregational Space', and 'Talk of a Town', before we move through 'National Proportions' and 'Span of a Continent' and arrive at 'Global Exchange' and 'Circumference of the Earth'. Then, we move back with 'Continental Ecosystems' and 'Community Dynamics' (395), eventually arriving at the final chapter entitled 'Perfect Female', in a playful take on the idea of a female *bildungsroman*. The novel thus mixes individual, local, and global scales as well as ecological and social plotlines (see Bartosch 2018).

Geographer and educator David Hicks (2015) has written about the need to help students to 'learn to see' climate change. Literary fiction is doing exactly that; in fact, the imaginative bridging of these different scales may well be one of the prime achievements of literary texts, as Scott Slovic points out:

> the human mind is tragically insensitive to large-scale phenomena. The change from one to two is more salient to us than the difference between thirty and thirty-one. By the time we're talking about 350 or 400 ppm of carbon dioxide in the atmosphere, the numbers wash right past us, causing virtually no affective response. Social scientists have identified and attached names to these various mental processes, but writers and artists have also intuited such cognitive limitations and have invented communication strategies (usually involving multidimensional combinations of abstract, quantitative overviews and salient,

individualized narratives or 'trans-scalar' movements between individual and collective representations of information) designed to strike home with audiences. This is where [. . .] the prospect of effective teaching of climate change literature comes into play. (2017, 164)

This brings us, finally, to *foregrounding*, a notion that draws on research in Gestalt psychology and formalist narratology and is now being employed in text processing psychology, among other fields. There, it could be shown that understanding relies to a large extent on 'variations of figure-ground discrimination during the reading process' (van Holt and Groeben 2005, 311), a cognitive operation that has also attracted attention in language and literature pedagogy (Carl et al. 2020). It could be said that cli-fi is defined by its foregrounding of climate in narrative; at the same time, it seems indisputable that cli-fi also foregrounds the human dimension of massive change on an earth-system scale. What matters to us is the quality of foregrounding at work in individual texts: *Flight Behaviour*, for instance, foregrounds its heroine and domestic concerns just as much as it points to the connection between climate change and biodiversity loss. One could even say that these concerns are deliberately '*backgrounded*' in the other texts, which in turn foreground other concerns – risk in *Odds against Tomorrow*, say, or family ties and relationships, including with flora, in *A Friend of the Earth*. This is important when we think about Hulme's assessment, discussed in the previous section, that 'imagining the future cannot be reduced to *climate* alone' (2021, 228). Not only do texts define and emplot figure and ground differently; texts that deliberately 'background' climate might even offer more insightful takes on climate change than those that expressly engage with climate change in its more familiar form as an earth-systemic phenomenon.

Foregrounding in our context may therefore also mean that a concept otherwise conspicuously absent from or largely implicit in a text suddenly assumes special significance once it *does* appear in a text. As an example, the notion of climate change is hardly explicitly mentioned in Bacigalupi's *The Windup Girl,* set in a far future Thailand, ruled by an oppressive government and biotech mega-corporations who control the world's food production after natural seeds have almost everywhere been replaced with genetically engineered crops. With catastrophes such as pandemics and pests regularly causing havoc to humans and nonhuman beings, the general sense of environmental destruction is pervasive throughout the novel and appears to hinge on an implicit sense that dramatic climate change lies behind it. Thus, a cluster of references, to 'the levee', 'the seawall', 'the physical defences that push pack the hungry sea', and to prayers 'for the continued life of their fragile city' (Bacigalupi 2009, 151), assume a significance they would hardly acquire in a text less centrally reliant on a sense of environmental degradation (cf. also Idema 2020). Especially regarding teaching situations and our understanding of stories as 'told for some purpose', it also matters that imaginative world building, and consecutive processes of fore- and backgrounding, all rely on readerly experience and expectation. As they activate their real-life knowledge to fill in gaps (see James 2022, 40–1), readers enter, as James writes, 'a complex dance of what is narrated in a narrative and the real-world contexts that allow authors and readers to produce and fill-in what is not, respectively' (41).

We are pointing to this because foregrounding can also be the result of reading a text in a new context. Contemporary readers of Boyle's *A Friend of the Earth*, first published in 2000, will surely read the following passages differently since the COVID-19 pandemic: 'Lori died in the *mucosa* epidemic that hit here three years ago. [...] Lori died in my arms, both of us wearing gauze masks, the *mucosa* so thick in her lungs and throat she couldn't draw a breath, tracheotomy or no, and that's natural, nothing more natural than the disease we spread in our sticky, promiscuous way. [...] We all wore masks and kept strictly to ourselves the last time' (Boyle 2000, 4; 73; 112). In this vein, a commentator on goodreads.com in June 2020 wrote: 'I do not recommend reading this during a pandemic! I had to put it aside because it was too depressing. Mucosa virus and masks? Eek! I'm not even sure why I pressed on to get through this book [...] I certainly didn't find the humour people keep mentioning in reviews here. Maybe it's there and too close to home at the moment so I couldn't see it?' ['Tanya', n.p]. Similarly, *Odds Against Tomorrow* has been read differently when extratextual events forced readers to recontextualise it: A reader recalls how startling it was to come across this novel, whose plot-driving risk scenario is the flooding of New York after a superstorm, after storm Sandy had hit the city: 'It was definitely sort of a Twilight Zone moment' (Evancie 2013, n.p). Such occurrences not only affect foregrounding, but they can lead to completely new forms of reception touching upon matters of readerly engagement, emotional impact, and processes of identification. These are the cues for our next section and for our suggestion of how to counter the sentimental fallacy: enter critical empathy.

More than 'Feeling With': Enter Critical Empathy

What we are calling the sentimental fallacy conceives of literary fiction as a vehicle to bring about appropriate affect in the hope that this, in turn, brings about appropriate action, whether by way of negative and alarming scenarios or in the more upbeat version of talking about climate solutions and presenting readers with environmental heroes that they can identify with. And just as with the cognitive fallacy, our point is one about complexity and contingency: we aren't saying that fiction does not affect us, just as we haven't said that we don't learn from reading. But we are convinced that the hope underlying the sentimental fallacy – that certain narratives lead to specific emotions in readers generally, and that this, in turn, inspires lasting behavioural change – underestimates both the complexity of literature and the contingency of readerly engagement with it. We nonetheless endorse the notion that empathy plays a big part in climate change literacy – only that we are conceiving of it as an aspect of critical thinking, built on textual negotiations of perspective and subsequent processes of identification.

The long-standing research history of literary empathy has resurfaced in the debate on climate change communication, where emotional storytelling is hoped to 'increase salience of climate change' and to make it 'more approachable and manageable' (Boykoff 2019, 106–7). With studies such as Suzanne Keen's *Empathy and the Novel* (2007) and Blakey Vermeule's *Why Do We Care about Literary Characters?* (2010), the study of narrative has helped establish a more nuanced understanding of literary empathy and of the technique narratology knows as 'focalisation'. In addition, recent work in the environmental humanities on 'strategic empathy' and affective engagements with literature and film has further underlined the importance as well as the intricacies of the 'affective ecologies' it allows for (Weik von Mossner 2017a). Not unlike the notion of discourse awareness, arguments about literary empathy and especially the objective to 'use readers' empathy strategically to make a moral argument' (78) resonate with pedagogical thinking, too. This is because perspective-taking and the task of understanding otherness (*Fremdverstehen*) are central to literary education and have even found their way into educational curricula (Volkmann 2015).

Dellarobia, the protagonist of *Flight Behaviour*, just like Laura in *The Carbon Diaries 2015*, indeed seems to invite sympathetic identification with many readers. Thus, in *Flight Behaviour*, in a more straightforward way than in any other text of our corpus, narrative focalisation on Dellarobia exerts what Magdalena Mączyńska describes as the text's 'pedagogical power': 'the reader learns alongside the protagonist, acquiring not only new terminology, but metacognitive insight into the processes of perception and learning' (2023, forthcoming). And yet, such straightforward appeals to identification are strikingly rare. Take T.C. Boyle's *A Friend of the Earth* (2000). The novel introduces us to Ty Tierwater, a 75-year-old monkey wrencher, who in a thoroughly climate-changed world takes care of a derelict private zoo's remaining animals, when he meets with his former wife, Andrea, and subsequently reminisces about their past as environmental activists, including the death of their daughter, Sierra, who had fallen off a tree she was trying to protect from logging.

A possible environmental hero alright – but here's how Ty describes Andrea when they reunite at the beginning of the novel: 'her eyes are paler and duller than I remembered – and ever so slightly exophthalmic – but who's to quibble? She was a beauty then and she's a beauty still' (Boyle 2000, 10). Tierwater's superficial, male gaze would not be too significant if it weren't for the fact that most novels from our corpus employ similar tendencies – the adulterous and often misogynistic Beard in *Solar* and the personnel of *Forty Signs of Rain* being obvious examples – and that we learn in numerous flashbacks and through Tierwater's memories in *A Friend of the Earth* that his desire to save the environment may only have been prompted by his desire to bed Andrea. This hardly makes him an inspiring eco-hero. What the novel offers instead is to point to the importance of *perspective*. Not only is Tierwater's own motivation to become an environmental activist crucially influenced by his desire to woo Andrea; once readers focus on the importance of perspectivised accounts over and against the more neutral voice we find in scientific reports, for instance, they might notice that the narrative creates two different forms of perspective: the story set in the 'now' of 2025 features a first-person account of Tierwater's experiences, thoughts, and feelings, while the flashbacks that relate Tierwater's and his family's earlier days are written in the third person. This is important for at least two reasons: it is key to understanding one central element of the story, namely the appearance of April Wind, who wants to write a book about the incidents in the 1980s – the second level of narrative. April interviews Andrea and Ty, but it is only as the narrative unfurls that readers learn about her ambition to write a biography – and have to start to wonder whether the third-person accounts they have been reading use this perspective because they are in fact part of said biography.

This, in turn, points to the importance of perspective in a more general sense and beyond the simple assumption of feeling-with a protagonist: novels might very well refrain from using likeable characters as focalisers and still achieve a great deal in thickening our understanding of climate change as a collective action problem, including a collectivity of unlike-minded people. The importance of perspective is also highlighted by a passage in *Solar*, in which Beard and his business associate Hammer are discussing their projected energy generation plant based on the ideas Beard has stolen from his postdoc. Trying to understand the different risks involved, Hammer asks Beard: 'Is it true, the planet's getting cooler? [. . .] If the place isn't hotting up, we're fucked' (296–7). Beard's response is illuminating:

'Here's the good news. The UN estimates that already a third of a million people a year are dying from climate change. Bangladesh is going down because the oceans are warming and expanding and rising. There's drought in the Amazonian rainforest. Methane is pouring out of the Siberian permafrost. There's a meltdown under the Greenland ice sheet that no one really wants to talk about. Amateur yachtsmen have been sailing the North-West Passage. Two years ago we lost forty per cent of the Arctic summer ice. Now the eastern Antarctic is going. The future has arrived, Toby.' [. . .] Beard laid a hand on his friend's arm, a sure sign that he was well over his limit [with drinks]. 'Toby, listen. It's a catastrophe, relax!' (298; see also Lehtimäki 2020, 97)

It is, of course, only from the perspective of someone intent on building a business based on the need for renewable energy because of climate change that the impending 'catastrophe' of global warming is 'good news' and a reason to 'relax'. Though entirely consistent, this is hardly a perspective readers will uncritically take over. And yet, it is necessary for a climate-literate person to understand that such perspectives exist and may even be crucial in the process of sustainability transformations.

Odds Against Tomorrow, a novel that with Mitchell Zukor features another protagonist not readily recognisable as an environmental hero, makes a similar point about perspective: focaliser Zukor is an anxiety-ridden doomster with a talent for maths whose constant expectation of catastrophe renders him first an outcast and later, after freak disasters hit New York and the rest of the USA in ever shorter intervals, a rich man. It would be beside the point to ponder whether the novel invites us to empathise with Zukor. Rather, we believe that it is by refraining from such easy moments of recognition and empathy that literature can underline the importance of perspective when '"performing" climate change', staging 'experiences, reactions and conflicts arising from it' as well as unsettling 'entrenched habits of thought, prompt[ing] self-awareness and trigger[ing] reflection' (Goodbody 2020, 321).

We might therefore be better advised to think about *perspectives*, in the plural. In pronounced contrast to scientific attempts at an impartial voice (aka 'facts and figures'), literary fiction thrives on subjectivity and idiosyncrasies. With an eye on the educational demand for 'viewpoint diversity' – 'the most crucial, and demanding form of difference to accommodate' in the literature classroom (Garrard 2021, 62) – we might follow Erin James's call for narratives about collective agency and we-narrators (2022, 156), or endorse Martin Puchner's similar demand for 'stories with collective agents' (2022, 97). But we also might look for moments in which narratives perform their own perspectivisation so blatantly that this performance invites, indeed necessitates, reflexion.

Thus, we maintain that processes of *identification* are critical to how cli-fi may function in climate change communication – if in a less straightforward manner than is commonly assumed. Rather, it fosters critical empathy. A case in point is again to be found in *Solar*: Though Myren-Svelstad rightly points out that '[r]eader responses are highly individual, and one reader's distaste for a perceived morally repulsive character does not preclude the possibility that other readers may construe the same character as a role model' (7), McEwan's protagonist Michael Beard is hard to see as anything but egotistical, deceitful, a notorious womaniser and irresponsible careerist, who harms himself by his undisciplined drinking and over-eating, very much against his better knowledge. However, the virtually universal distaste he engenders in readers seems to be precisely the point: Garrard has even argued that Beard's 'grotesque body' is central to the novel's 'satirical allegory' (2013, 125; 130). As Richard Kerridge observed in an early perceptive comment on the novel, '[Beard's] failure to restrain or change his appetites for the sake of long-term well-being [...] represents the collective failing of wealthy consumers to change their behaviour in response to the threat of global warming' (2010, 155). Beard thus functions as a sort of representative 'Everyman'; we might speak of a form of critical identification in that we may see ourselves in Beard and will, ideally, seek to avoid his failings (see also Hoydis 2019, 537–54).

This means that identification does take place but might be happening in more complex and contradictory ways than the cheering for a personable character. In her early landmark study on empathy, Keen (2007) pointed out the intricacies of identification and empathy, especially regarding the fact that 'readers most readily empathize with their in-group which it is the easiest for them to identify', as James (2022, 36) summarises the research (see Keen 2007, 11; and Schneider-Mayerson 2020). To move beyond that frame, we are taking our cue from postcolonial scholar Gayatri Chakravorty Spivak's notion of 'counter-focalisation': writing about subjects who are 'resolutely denied focalisation' at the expense of unlikeable, disagreeable protagonists, she wonders what this does to the reading experience since '[n]o reader is content with acting out the failure of the reading' (2012, 323). She suggests readers are encouraged to 'counter-focalise', that is, to imagine the unheard perspective just as to probe the possibilities of identification beyond facile sympathetic connections. Literature, she avers, thus helps us 'to imagine the other who does not resemble the self' (324).

This is key in intercultural education with literature but should also inform debates on climate change literacy since dissent, controversy, and conflict will surely be among the main characteristics of the coming 'everything change' (Atwood) that we need to better accommodate if we want to forego what Isabell Stengers calls 'the coming barbarism' (2015; see also Bartosch 2021). It would then indeed be possible to read novels such as *Solar* as 'valuable models of how *not* to behave' (James 2022, 58), or to agree with Boyle's Ty Tierwater on the cognitive and emotional costs of perspective-taking: 'I try to avoid perspective as much as possible. Perspective hurts. Live in the present, that's what I say, one step at a time, and forget nostalgia, forget history, forget the sketchy chain of loss, attrition and disappointment that got you into bed last night and out of it this morning' (Boyle 2000, 111). A climate-change-literate person, however, cannot overlook and in fact relishes the diversity of perspective and fiction's creative forms of bringing about the 'loss of familiar habits of thought and representation to pave the way for creative alternatives' (Braidotti 2013, 88–9).

The Windup Girl, to conclude with a final example, also lends itself to showing how cli-fi texts involve readers in such complex forms of perspective-taking, though again not, as is often assumed, by making them take the perspective of likeable climate scientists or activists. Rather, before readers have acquired a fuller sense of the complex constellation of characters and of their ethical orientations, through consistent internal focalisation for the first thirty pages of the novel, they are led to identify with Anderson Lake. As it turns out, he is the international agritech executive out to destroy Thailand's crop diversity and to lay his hands on the country's wealth of non-engineered crop seeds. To be led to identify with 'the wrong person' and to be enlightened during the reading engagement is a highly effective educational process, as Stanley Fish famously argued in the 1960s (Fish [1967] 1998). And it points to the relevance of perceptive and receptive processes receiving great attention in cognitive literary studies and poetics, including contagion (Plantinga 1999), transportation (Martínez 2018), and narrative resonance (Seilman and Larsen 1989), and their effective critical contestation through narrative form.

Hardly any of the widely discussed cli-fi novels provide persuasive role models for readers to emulate; and climate-conscious behaviour is generally portrayed as the result of questionable motivations such as impressing women, career advancement, or financial gain. Meanwhile, risk awareness in the case of Mitchell Zukor in *Odds Against Tomorrow* appears excessive, even patho-logical, rather than responsible. We therefore need to pay more attention to 'critical empathy'. Critical empathy still relies on transportation, perspective-taking, and emotional contagion – these are cognitive-affective results of processes of reception that cannot be done away with and continue to be relevant for the immersive experience of reading. However, these processes do not have to be linked with desirable behaviours, by fictional characters and their readers, or with agreement and approval. Instead, it is high time we cultivate forms of critical empathy that allow us 'to imagine the other who does not resemble the self'.

More than Climate: Enter Systems Thinking

Looking into our corpus of popular cli-fi so far has underlined that literary fiction goes a long way in providing insights into the discursive construction of climate change. It also produces more critical forms of empathetic engagement with fictional characters than the cognitive and sentimental fallacies suggest. This has led us to argue that discourse awareness and critical empathy constitute core elements of climate change literacy. Writing about these specific literary affordances as we have done so far has pointed us to a problem of systematising literary writing along these lines, however: while heuristically helpful, clear-cut distinctions between moments of framing and scaling, between foregrounding techniques and readerly reception of characters and the development of critical empathy and so forth are hard to maintain. This is neither coincidental nor, we believe, a fault in our readings. Rather, it appears that cli-fi comes into its own when it links scientific concerns with climate to the complexity of individual and societal human factors. Whereas scientific modelling of climate change has a hard time accounting for such human factors (Bonneuil and Fressoz 2013, 32–4) and uses storytelling in the limited sense of what Lieven Ameel calls 'fraught fictionality' (2021), the texts we have engaged with in their various ways present us with a more-than-scientific, intersectional approach to climate change, enmeshed as it is with – in fact, constituted by – societal aspects through and through.

We propose to understand the narrativisation of climate intersectionality in terms of 'socio-ecological complexity' and suggest the environmental humanities make good use of this specific literary affordance, especially considering demands, in climate change communication research and sustainability education alike, for better understandings of complexity and greater literacy in systems thinking. With Andrew Stirling, these demands can be summarised as calls to 'keep it complex' (2010), demands that have a prominent place in educational policies as well (UNESCO's 'systems thinking competency' comes to mind just like global learning's concern with agency in complex global situations). *Forty Signs of Rain* frames climate change as a political challenge and not only links it with state and research politics, but includes different viewpoints from various characters with diverging cultural, socioeconomic and gender biographies. *Flight Behaviour* excels in linking domestic and ecological scales and presents a female perspective over and against an otherwise prevalent male gaze in cli-fi personnel (think *Solar* and *A Friend of the Earth*). Thus, these texts' head-on engagements with socio-ecological complexities provide better access to reflections on agency and the (in)ability of individuals and communities to react appropriately than other, less heteroglot accounts of climate change.

In a sense, socio-ecological complexity plays into both discourse awareness and critical empathy, or rather serves as a counterpoint to the cognitive and sentimental fallacies. Instead of climate knowledge, readers learn about complex entanglements; instead of feeling with likeable characters or fearing imminent cataclysms, they experience what has been described as moments of 'anagnorisis' (Bruhn 2019; Bergthaller 2021) – a moment, that is, of the 'concrete realization' of a supposedly abstract reality of climate change as a thoroughly everyday phenomenon linked with and co-dependent on other everyday concerns. Therefore, *Odds Against Tomorrow* is at least as much a novel about risk perception, fear, and corporate capitalism as it is about climate disaster and health. Its curious mix of climate catastrophe and risk managerialism points to this, discursively displayed either in terminology – 'Event trees, optimism bias, binomial distribution, base rate fallacy' (Rich 2013, 13) – or in formulas such as '$\lambda_{CMTC} = \lambda_{IE}P_1P_2P_3$' without further explanation (73). As do references to corporate lingo and, as was the case in *Solar*, the paradoxical pleasure in disaster by those benefitting from crises: '"Where is [the hurricane] going to make landfall? [...] Ocean City would be very bad – Atlantic City would be catastrophic." "Let's pray for Atlantic City!"' (88).

Interestingly, *Forty Signs of Rain* not only tells us about the mechanisms and problems of science funding in the US and about political machinations, but moreover and through the fictitious island country of Kembalung and the 'League of Drowning Nations' seeks to give voice to a Global South perspective, if not at all fully successfully. Questions of justice loom large in several of our texts and thus point to one of the central challenges of socio-ecological complexity: environmental justice. Whereas scientific accounts of climate change primarily endorse a descriptive register and have a hard time including normative issues in their calculations, novels such as *Flight Behaviour* show that concerns of justice are always central when it comes to environmental crises, especially regarding poverty and vulnerability. Exploring class, gender roles and education in a conservative rural community and urban-rural divides in the US, the novel dramatises the correlation between poverty and sustainability and between wealth and excessive resource consumption: When Dellarobia goes through 'a list of things you promise to do to lower your carbon footprint' (450), it becomes clear that she does virtually all of these things – such as reducing food waste, not buying bottled water, buying recycled or reused products, avoiding flights – but not in order to reduce her carbon footprint but simply out of the need to save money. Accordingly, Milkoreit writes, the novel engages with 'the social realities that have created America's political culture around climate change today', including the recognition that current technical solutions to the climate crisis, 'from carbon accounting and reduction to renewable power, feed-in tariffs and carbon markets', remain oblivious to and leave intact the structural and normative dimensions that shape (US as well as any other) society: 'family loyalties, identity commitments, value and belief systems, human motivations, and systemic constraints of human behavior, including poverty, lack of education and choice' (2016, 181).

These readings support an understanding of fiction as an imaginary arena that invariably couples climate-related concerns with human ones, both in the context of language and discourse and in the case of human drama, cultural dynamics, and ethics. We therefore believe that cli-fi lends itself to exploring complex socio-ecological issues and questions of environmental justice. By virtue of its intersectional take on climate, it forcefully underlines that 'climate change isn't a traditional antagonist. It can't be stopped by a hero with a bullet or a clever ruse. The forces that drive it are deeply systemic' (Brady 2019).

Discourse awareness, critical empathy, and socio-ecological complexity: we've come a long way from the faulty assumption that fiction can be a handmaiden to science communication to now identifying and cherishing the unique potentials of literature to thickening understanding. An approach to climate change literacy that builds on these potentials echoes Myren-Svelstad's assertion that literature can play a vital role in helping to handle the complexity of the phenomenon of climate change, 'not because it provides us with models for pro-environmental behavior, but because learning to read literature competently entails learning to critically evaluate and re-evaluate opinions, postponing con-clusions, and acknowledging that several diverging viewpoints can be reasonable at the same time' (2020, 17). Especially since literary and cultural education has for a long time been concerned with discourse, empathy, and complexity, we are confident that reading literature has a place in the English classroom as well as in debates in the environmental humanities and in climate change communication, to which it adds important and robust insights. As we outline below, however, our readings and their attention to the specificity of individual texts also second the notion that 'climate fiction [...] needs to be more of a diverse and situated practice' (Ismail 2022, 15). This is true because of the biases of the cli-fi canon, discussed above. But it is also true because the diverse and situated practice of reading plays out very differently in individual readers – an insight every educator had better take seriously and include in a framework of climate change literacy such as the one suggested here. It is with this in mind that we turn from literature to literacy environments in the next section.

3 Literacy Environments

Undoubtedly, *literature* environments matter. But climate change literacy remains insufficiently conceptualised without careful considerations of what we propose to call *literacy* environments: the environs in which acts of reading take place. It is these environments that engender meaningful, transformative relations with literary fiction and thus now complement our readings in the previous section. For this, we look at research in ecopedagogies and on processes of literary learning to move beyond the question what literature can do and towards a better understanding of what can be done with literature. The section is organised around three main concerns about 'texts', 'textures', and 'tasks', for which we suggest '3Ts' as a shorthand. These operate in, and at the same time create, literacy environments – the space in which literacy practices are enacted and cultivated, and the space in which the sometimes abstract and always intangible nature of fiction can become a lived reality. It is by way of these 3Ts that we seek to do equal justice to the diversity of literary narratives and imaginaries, and to the diversity of learners, their demands as well as their capabilities.

Turning literary fiction into a part of lived reality is what distinguishes the mere ability to read from fiction having a meaningful role in the lives of readers and the context of climate change (and, indeed, elsewhere). Researchers like Matthis Kepser have shown that lived media realities are made of various media formats and ways of engaging with them, and that these ways of engagement touch upon different levels of individual enculturation, group-related socialisation, as well as macro-level cultural activity more generally. Kepser and Abraham therefore speak of a 'field of action' and a practice rather than an object of inquiry when discussing literature in educational contexts: Literature pedagogy, they say, is about enabling and empowering learners to participate in this multidimensional forcefield of literary practices (2016, 69). Understanding literacy practices as matters of such meaningful participation should be key in climate-related educational discussion: As Harald Welzer notes, modern media ecologies include lived fictions of comfortable consumption and greenwashed progress that all-too often compete with the bleak cautionary tales of collapse and surrender that still make for much of cli-fi. Unlike complex cautionary tales, these stories can be enacted and enlivened in the present – just order something on the internet, and enjoy the stuff you bought, without second thoughts, the next day (cf. Welzer and Turiak). How can climate fiction make a difference over and against the seductive, ahistorical as well as afuturical fund of such stories? This is no rhetorical question – it is a research problem for literature pedagogy.

We believe it is all about creating literacy environments that are lived realities within the practice field of literature. To get there, we must return to what we have said about literacy research in the first section and consider in which ways literacy is recognised as a key component of successful educational efforts. On one hand, there is a wealth of studies focused on individuals' abilities to read and write and on empirically assessing pedagogical interventions concerning the improvement of literacy (e.g., Center 2020; Diehr and Rymarczyk 2015). On the other hand, while these mostly quantitative studies proliferate data on specific literacy skills in ever greater numbers, discussions about literacy increasingly tend to emphasise the critical dimension of literacy: concepts such as futures literacy, health literacy or science literacy expressly move beyond an understanding of literacy as a skill of decoding and point to an individual's ability to assess information and act upon it (see, e.g., Carneiro and Gordon 2013). As Rahat Naqvi notes: 'To be critically literate is to be able to do more than produce and represent information [. . .]. The aim is the development of human capacity to use texts to analyse and transform social relations and material conditions' (2015, 50). This is what connects literacy research with other educational efforts in global learning, sustainability, or future literacies contexts. It also underlines a demand for critical as well as creative ways of engaging fictional worldmaking.

The connection between basic and critical literacy is sometimes described as a continuum; sometimes it is simply assumed that one follows from the other. The most helpful studies, often in the field of so-called New Literacy – or New Literacies – Studies, point to the social, rather than the merely psychological dimensions of literacy, and thus link the critical with practices of reading, relationships between readers and texts, and cultural contexts more broadly (Gee 2015). But where does this leave the literary text? Section 2 spelled out what we consider literature's unique contributions to understanding and engaging with climate change, especially concerning the role of discourse awareness and critical empathy, as well as the challenges of complexity and systems thinking – so far, however, without systematically explaining what we can do with this insight in the process of engendering literacy environments. A brief look at educational theory and policy suggests that this would be both possible and desirable, as discourse, empathy, and complexity loom large as pedagogical challenges that urgently need to be addressed. It seems high time to recognise that works on language awareness (James and Garrett 1995) and literary learning share an interest in discourse competence. Or that studies on reading and empathy (e.g., Keen 2007) begin to acknowledge and research the transformative role of education and literary socialisation (Bortolussi and Dixon 1996; Fialho 2019). Consilient exchange on these matters might go a long way in showing how literature brings about understandings of complexity and lends itself to critical thinking in a way that also fosters climate change literacy.

Besides individual studies in sustainability or environmental education and related fields (Parham 2006; Eppelsheimer et al. 2015; Bartosch 2021), prominent stakeholders such as UNESCO demand educational efforts to be directed towards these challenges as well, most prominently in the Sustainable Development Goals catalogue, especially with the demand for 'climate action' and 'quality education'. We welcome the fact that regarding climate action, primarily science-centred debates about sustainability in education have shifted to embracing a broader understanding, including the role of language, culture, values, and the complexities of socio-ecological crises. This understanding productively links education in language, literature, and culture with demands for sustainable and transformative learning, highlighting values, meaning, and purpose. Sustainability transformations require these aspects just as much as they are drawing on technological, scientific, and legal resources. Consequently, quality education then can be conceived of as 'the teaching and learning of a set of literacy practices and the cultural ideologies and fields that a particular set of literacy practices index' (Bloome and Green 2015, 21). This means that quality education in literature and culture for climate action must cultivate such practices and for this must tap into the full potential of literary texts in order to underline the significance and value of Boykoff's 'creative communications'. Viewing literature as creative communication facilitates rethinking the role and potential of literary learning, but also caters to literacy and diversity in heterogeneous classrooms. With this in mind, we approach climate change literacy more systematically by way of our three Ts: Texts, Textures, and Tasks.

However, while systematic distinctions help as heuristics, they don't work as deep conceptual trenches: Climate change literacy results from the genuine interplay of what we are calling texts, textures, and tasks. Texts matter but are only part of the story, as educators aren't the only ones to readily acknowledge. Scholars in the aesthetics of reception and literature pedagogy, such as Wolfgang Iser or Louise Rosenblatt, have also shown that it is only in acts of reading that a literary text is 'concretised'. These acts we call literacy practices, situated in specific literacy environments, and linked with appropriate task designs. Roberto Careiro and Jean Gordon understand the creation of such environments as one of the key objectives for better literacy education (2013, 493) as they afford what Nathan Snaza calls 'literacy situations' and 'literacy events': 'moments when literacy practices operate in ways that generate meaning of many kinds' (2019, 17). This meaning – particularly in its 'many kinds' – exists or must be made to extend beyond the merely analytical level of textual interpretation. It helps to recall that literature education always 'takes place in a complex ecology of both sociocultural and physical factors, of texts, readers, teachers, educational policy documents, and classrooms' (Myren-Svelstad 2020, 7) and to proceed accordingly when teaching literary fiction. This includes more than just the selection of a text and the formulation of analytical questions: it matters, for instance, what readers know and can do already, which age group they belong to, or in which contexts literary texts are encountered and to what end. In analogy to James's definition of narrative as '*somebody telling someone else on some occasion and for some purpose(s) that something happened in some world*' (2022, 28), we can thus conceive of teaching narratives as somebody guiding someone else for some purpose to see that something happened in some – and indeed in our – world.

An example of the importance of thinking about *literacy* environments in connection with *literature* environments in the case of climate action and quality education can be found in Schneider-Mayerson's qualitative studies that we have referred to throughout this Element. In his discussion of Rich's *Odds Against Tomorrow* and its reception by literary scholars, Schneider-Mayerson notes, '[m]ost critics applauded *Odds Against Tomorrow*, contending that it describes and examines the "modern condition" (Evancie) and the future of "human communities" (Newitz) in the era of climate change' (2019, 950). His own reading differs significantly, for he takes issue with the fact that the novel's main characters are exclusively white, young, educated, and mobile, and he points to the absence of justice and global majority perspectives. We find interesting that his recent survey of American readers of climate fiction shows that the debate whether Rich's novel is borderline racist or a clever satire on structural racism was altogether lost on flesh-and-blood, non-academic readers:

> none of the readers of *Odds Against Tomorrow* appeared to view the novel as satire, and some reported that its primary lesson concerned the need for personal disaster preparedness. [...] At least one reader seemed to view [the protagonist] as a model for climate adaption [...] Similarly, an analysis of 50 randomly selected reviews of the novel posted on the website Goodreads shows that while a minority of readers considered *Odds Against Tomorrow* to be satire, most did not. (Schneider-Mayerson 2019, 951)

This finding calls for stating the obvious. How texts (climate fictions) are being read is a matter of education, of being literate in the very specific sense of being capable of 'aesthetic reading' (borrowing Rosenblatt's term). Surprisingly, this basic fact is all too often overlooked, especially in the context of literary scholarship. While it happily embraces cognitive and empirical theory and research methodology, it remains (mostly) blissfully unaware of the fact that being able to read is closely tied to practices of reading, in informal but most importantly in formal educational settings. The environmental humanities, and ecocritical theory especially, can and should be a valuable exception, both because of their concern with transdisciplinary, societal impact and because, as Garrard reminds us, ecocriticism 'has been preoccupied with pedagogy since its inception' (2012, 1). A similar preoccupation would be needed in climate change communication research, which, while it does pay attention to different audiences and their needs and abilities, has shown less interest in the role of fiction, aesthetics, and imaginaries.

Even researchers as perceptive and attentive to the empirical situation of actual readers as Alexa Weik von Mossner tend to overlook this educational dimension of literacy: In a study on the 'affective dimensions of risk in young adult cli-fi' (Weik von Mossner 2017b), she engages with the question in how far cautionary and apocalyptic tales can incite action or at least reading pleasure. For this, she discusses the value of 'cognitive estrangement' and 'liberated embodied simulation' (2017b, 555; 556) to make sense of the weird pleasure of reading disaster narratives and potentially moving 'from estrangement to engagement' (555). However, her theoretically informed reading of YA cli-fi makes a case for literary learning that falls short of literacy environments. This leads her to assume ecological knowledge to play a greater part than literacy practices with which any kind of knowledge is being negotiated collectively and collaboratively in educational settings. Acceding that reading pleasure derives mostly from dramatic plotlines rather than the ecological dimensions of such texts, she points out that even with literature that is not 'overly didactic', readers may 'learn about tar sand development and "carbon production limits," about sea level rise and "people dying from draught"' (560). Her choice of words is telling. The novel, she says, 'sneak[s] in a few lessons about the relationship between unbridled capitalism, carbon emissions, and environmental devasta-tion' (560). Literary reading is about such connections, especially in the case of cli-fi, that is, in narratives written by people with an express interest in making a case or bringing home an ethical point about crisis and catastrophe. Yet our conception of climate change literacy modifies the argument that it is primarily the texts themselves or these authors that 'sneak in the lessons' – or that it is these lessons that ultimately matter. Rather, the lessons we are imagining are provided by reading experiences in literacy environments. Many discussions of the affective impact of cli-fi fall short of accounting for these experiences because they *only* focus on the textual dimension of fiction. Our take on climate change literacy, however, is as much centred on the uniqueness of literary texts as it is on readerly relations engendered in the act of reading. These relations are created in literacy environments, and we are convinced that education for sustainability and climate change communication research interested in the role and potential of fiction need to take this aspect of literacy seriously.

Texts

Understanding literacy relationally doesn't diminish the significance of the texts themselves. Literature environments rather link directly with the component of *texts*, the first 'T'. Yet in this context, the matter is one of justified selection and, therefore, of literary quality – although not in the sense of supposedly timeless aesthetic judgements but in the functional sense of linking *qualia* and textual specificity. Critical literacy always entails a problematic challenge of normativity, as Naqvi, cited above, has noted. For us, however, the question of what makes a text – in other words, its quality – doesn't mean we suggest selecting texts for their ideological value or their authors' ingenious ways with language but look at them as specific avenues into storyworlds that consequently afford specific literature environments. Literature provides a take on climate change that differs from scientific and other narratives – but individual texts do so in specific and different ways. If we want to make use of literature's potential for allowing more diverse understandings of climate change, we need to think about literature environments and their respective affordances – and why they could matter to learners engaging with them. It is this dimension of a text's unique quality that counts. This in fact implies that any myopically normative focus on quality would be misplaced, for as Matt Bell writes, '[t]here are as many ways to write climate fiction as there are experiences of the climate crisis' (2021, 101).

Yet, if there are in fact many ways to write climate fiction, as Bell and many others remind us, the dimension of 'text' not only points to the specificity of literature but to the specificity of the individual literary text – for its own sake as much as in relation to other texts. Section 2 has shown how, with these texts, it is not only a matter of literary engagement with climate change, but of the various ways in which literature allows and stages such engagement. *Solar* operates with humour and thus provides moments of critical empathy as well as fore- and backgrounding of scientific voices in climate debates, while *Flight Behaviour* recontextualises climate change in gender and class debates, and uses literary form to point to the relevance of scale. In their various ways, these texts not only show that it is not enough to expect literature to provide information or offer slick emotional identification. Rather, it is through their respective singularity that texts provide privileged access to rethinking discourse and developing discourse awareness, move beyond feeling-with to foster critical empathy instead, and to always situate climate change in the socio-ecological environments from which it has come. They thus offer a notion of climate change as always and foundationally embedded and entangled – in other words, they stage complexity and thicken understanding.

This is helpful to keep in mind while thinking of literacy events, for this is where we see that the specific affordances of individual texts matter. It also helps to recall works in literary studies suggesting that literature and, indeed, individual texts constitute singular 'events' (Attridge 2004; Eagleton 2013). Mario Ortiz Robles, for instance, locates the character of this event on different levels of the text that make up what he calls its 'performativity': Drawing on

J. Hillis Miller, he names the 'positioning of the story', the 'testimony of the imagined narrator', the 'lives of the characters', and the readerly response (2010, 12; see also Miller 2005). Literary texts have something particular to say on these levels about climate change, discourse, perspective and empathy, and complexity. This also applies to *The Carbon Diaries 2015*, the novel we now draw on to illustrate the connection between literature and literacy environments: It is a *literary* text that engages with climate change; but it is also a *specific* literary text with *specific* potentials for climate change literacy. In the typical vein of young adult fiction, but with the additional benefit of showing the enmeshment of climate catastrophe and politics with the daunting challenges of adolescence, *The Carbon Diaries 2015* presents moments of systems thinking that might be particularly relevant for younger learners in the context of their literacy development: 'Everything is falling to pieces: my home, [the relationship with long-term best friend] Ravi – and now the band. Rationing has really dicked all over my life' (Lloyd 2008, 110).

The Carbon Diaries 2015, first published in 2008, tells the story of adolescent Laura who, together with her family and friends, experiences a new energy regime take hold of the lives of Londoners in a – then futuristic – year 2015. The UK introduces a 'carbon card' with which people are forced to track their consumption and which blocks carbon emissions once they exceed allocated levels. This plot takes place against the backdrop of spiralling climatic crises, in Europe and elsewhere, and the unravelling of urban life and modern Western ways of living. It subsequently presents processes of adaptation, acceptance, yet also responses of despair and anger. Typical of a YA novel, yet particularly significant for our argument, it also includes other concerns – fights with the family, falling in love, and struggling at school – that are constantly brought into conversation with the new reality of forced carbon reduction and civilisational collapse. If we follow Ortiz Robles in looking for the specific performativity of the text on the levels of story, narration, figures, and ways of readerly reception, we see how the text performs climate change's entanglement with adolescent, Western lifeways: It is positioned as a coming-of-age story in a time of unravelling; the narrator is speaking from the first-person singular and relates her experience by way of diary entries, thus staging authenticity and perspective as well as giving voice to anger and despair (see Marks et al. 2021) while simultaneously underlining discursive framing. It furthermore matters, when it comes to questions of empathy and complexity, that the *characters* of the story react differently, based on age, gender, sexuality, and many other factors. In addition, readerly response will be affected by who speaks and who sees within the story, as well as by the text's references to pop culture. These include the fact that the narrator and her friend are in a rock band, that the narrator's sister desperately wants to go on holiday by plane, or that the narrator's neighbour sees the climate catastrophe as an opportunity for creating a new dating app, based on carbon rationing above all else. The specificity of the text – its singularity – consists in the combination of the tone and concerns of young adult fiction and the depiction of the rationing regime through which it helps readers encounter a possible climate future. It furthermore does other things the cli-fi texts mentioned so far don't do: for instance, it presents the story in multimodal fashion, by presenting the story in different fonts, indicating differ-ent media of writing, and by including visualisations, such as mock photographs and scraggy notes from school lessons. With multimodality being all the rage in both current language and literature teaching research and in climate change communication (see Hallet 2018; Boykoff 2019, 215), there is good reason to take this specialty seriously. Before we discuss it in relation to climate change literacy, however, we come to the second T: Textures.

Textures

Let us return to the idea, discussed by Kepser and others, that being literate today includes the proficiency to move within the 'practice field of literature'. For literature to play a meaningful role, they argue, it needs to be situated within the lived realities of learners. Both insights, about the situatedness of literature within a field of practice and about the necessity of situating literary writing within readerly lifeworlds, have direct bearing on literacy environments. For one, this shows that the question about the 'best' cli-fi text is somewhat misguided – not only in the context of academic inquiry into narrative fiction, as discussed previously, but also and especially in the field of education: Looking for an exemplary text that does justice to the complexity of climate change may be laudable, yet eventually hopeless. If reading takes place within an ecology of reading and meaning, it is through the creation of environments made up of *different* texts and their specific vantages that the practice field of literature can be traversed. Only if we have made up our mind about a text's specific quality can we think about ways of arranging several such texts into differentiated, multiperspective and multimodal text ensembles that better represent the variety of literary ways of worldmaking as well as readerly forms of potential engagement. This is what we mean by textures.

To give just one example: the notion of scale, and the scaling of perspectives (see Section 2) is a mental activity needed for the interpretation of fiction as well as for making sense of climate change. But in the context of literacy and transformative change, it matters that it can be learned and practiced in different ways and with the aid of different texts (Bartosch 2021). *The Carbon Diaries* explicitly invokes a personal scale when presenting us with a first-person narrator and her diary; it brings in the scale of culture and community when carbon rationing is described as a national political act, in conflict with but maybe also spearheading other countries' policies. And it forcefully juxtaposes the more personal and the ecological when, discussing whether to cancel their long-awaited little tour, members of Laura's band pit musical expression against precipitation: 'You're cancelling? The country needs this message'. 'Mia, the country don't need a message, it needs rain' (Lloyd 2008, 225).

And yet, what matters is the ability and willingness to use the perception of scale in the everyday lifeworld, and for this, it matters if the text that has been used to cultivate this ability is meaningful and catering to an individual's imagination. As Moore and Milkoreit note, the imagination is a crucial component of trans- formative change as it 'provides the alternatives to reality that can motivate a reordering of the way things currently exist' (2020, 3). And they continue: 'To understand the causal power of the imagination, it is important to connect the individual scale – my imaginations of my future and its consequences for my behaviour – and the collective scale' (flagging). When thinking about how these two understandings of scale relate, and how this would (have to) influence the design of literacy environments, a text can be explored and scrutinised with different scales in mind – one can read for character agency, or cultural commu- nity behaviour, or planetary and ecological changes. Yet what is more, different texts aiming at different scales can be discussed in a way that brings about collective work on diverging scales. This would mean combining a text such as *The Carbon Diaries* with an array of other texts – other stories for sure, but also poetry and song, newspaper articles and visual media – that all scale in their different ways and forms and thus enrich classroom discussions revolving around the notion of scale in a much more inclusive and diverse manner. Ultimately, such an approach to scale, and thus to climate change literacy, better acknowledges that '[i]magination is both an individual-cognitive process, taking place in the brain, and a collective-social process that relies on communication and interaction between people but also between people and nature' (Milkoreit 2016, 174).

This diversity makes the texture of literacy environments. We take our inspiration – and, in fact, the term, texture – from research in literary studies and cognitive poetics. Peter Stockwell, for instance, defines 'texture' as the 'sense of textuality' (2012, 5) and the 'experiential quality of textuality' (14). Christoph Reinfandt calls texture a 'key term in literary and cultural studies' and claims that it provides access to 'the cumulative sedimentations of media evolution in which [modern culture] is grounded' (2013, 15). Although he speaks from within a quite different critical tradition, his concept of 'textures of modernity' is helpful for a discussion of the cultural work of cli-fi as well as its educational potential. The same is true for his notion of the text as offer and affordance (Reinfandt 2020). This idea links the text and its mediality, but it also includes 'an array of perceptual data' that an individual takes in and that informs meaning-making (2020, 16). This is for him 'the point of access for the reader' (18): by virtue of textures, 'acts of reading are better conceived as an entanglement of material form [. . .] and immaterial processes of signification' (455; our translation). Textures therefore realise a 'dynamic character of invitation and empowerment' (455) that matters in a literacy situation and with regard to a diversified understanding of climate change literacy. Each individual text's invitation and empowerment are different. Combining them in the form of textures offers the most diversified and therefore authentic literacy event.

With all we know from reader reception studies, the qualitative experience of textuality in actual readers is as diverse as the potentials of individual texts for providing such experience. Therefore, we suggest conceiving of textuality as a quality of multiple texts, each with their different and multiple affordances, in a rich semiotic environment that is organised like the larger practice field that literature pedagogy seeks to bring home to learners. A miniature or model literary field, if you will, that will yield better insights into the multifaceted ways of knowing, feeling, and speaking or writing about climate change, and one that offers more diverse entrances into climate change literacy for more diverse groups of learners. For this reason, it is helpful to reflect on a tradition in literature pedagogy that has focused on what has been called 'text ensembles' (Volkmann 2010, 255): like the notion of texture, text ensembles are made of a wide array of different texts, underlining that the practice field of literature is more and has to be more than a single text that would have to fulfil an unlikely, and potentially undesirable, one-size-fits-all job. The term 'texture' adds to this by underlining the qualitative experience of textuality as not only a matter of educational concern with learner abilities, but of the aesthetic potential of literary fiction(s).

It is the task of an educator to identify texts and their potentials and then to curate text ensembles that provide texture to climate change literacy environments. Thinking about textures therefore requires a concern with the specific potentials of texts as much as with individual learners' expectations and abilities as well as their situatedness in socio-ecological realities on several counts – including gender, class, ethnicity, cultural biography, and many more. Thankfully, as we have described above, the literary texts themselves offer leeway for such an inclusive view as they, too, provide experiences of entanglements in just the same way as are found in the literary classroom. For textures to become entangled with the lived realities of learners and to thus begin to matter, a third and final step is needed, however: that of task design. While literature prefigures entanglements of the kind that potentially advances better understandings of complexity, in addition to avenues for discourse awareness and critical empathy, tasks can integrate these components into meaningful conversations.

Tasks

Climate change literacy doesn't stop at selecting, creating, or designing textures. It matters not only *what* we read but *how* we deal with what we are reading (Myren-Svelstad 2020, 14). Research on task-based learning and teaching has shown that task design is key when it comes to meaningful and inclusive communicative teaching, and therefore, too, that it matters when teaching literature. The challenge lies in turning an abstract literary storyworld into a lived reality of learners. Climate fiction and narratives of sustainability don't exist in a vacuum but are competing with the lived realities of narratives of progress and consumption. Even the best alternative worlds can seem bloodless against the richness of unsustainable storytelling all around us – think of the example of online shopping at the beginning of this section. Literacy environments are therefore not just about exploring fictional worlds but about creating bridges into student life worlds – by way of meaningful discussions of the texts, or by indulging the imaginative power of images and ideas that change readerly perception for good. If, as we have shown above, literary fiction does a particularly good job achieving this by engendering discourse awareness or fostering critical empathy and an understanding of complex socio-ecological realities, it seems only logical that task design pay attention to this. It has been noted that research on sustainability education and literary learning continues to suggest educators focus on the transmission of environmental knowledge (cf. Celis-Diez et al. 2016) or the hope that students simply become more empathetic through reading (Bal and Veldkamp 2013) and change their behaviour (Echterling 2016), however. There is, of course, nothing wrong with either knowing or feeling things. But it is up to us, as educators and creators of literacy environments, to stress that unlike the IPCC's climate scenarios, the scenarios developed by fiction are highly and ambiguously complex, emergent, and in need of collaborative explorations. Instead of facile hope for behavioural change, we now have another argument for the thickening of understanding. Only by focusing on the diversity of texts, textures, and tasks might these explorations successfully bring about forms of climate change literacy thriving on the unique affordances of literary fiction.

Two scenes in *The Carbon Diaries 2015* serve to illustrate our point about tasks. In the first, Laura recalls in her diary that her mom tells Laura's sister off after having received a phone call from the Carbon Department. The mother learns about her carbon overshoot and shouts: 'I am really, really angry with you right now, Kimberley Brown! This is not just your life'. To which the daughter snaps back: 'I am really, really angry with you right now, Julia Brown! Cos of you I don't have a life' (Lloyd 2008, 68). This scene allows for discussions of carbon knowledge as well as empathy – but it also invites more complex engagements with intergenerational (in)justice and anger (see Bartosch 2022) in which learners can reflect on their own future impoverishment. A proper task will also allow for discussions of how language and complexity are relevant for understanding the conflict and its discursive staging. This needs a text like *The Carbon Diaries*; a mere discussion of carbon consumption could be had without it. In another scene, Laura and her friends watch a film together – with the right task design, this passage, too, can be turned into a moment of reflection. It nicely comments on how the media frame climate change and how literature tends to comment on these forms of framing in its own discourse: 'After practice, we all went to watch Icebreaker, which was this 3-D thriller about New York freezing over. It was kind of weird watching it though; it was meant to be all tear-jerky – this family and all the shit they were going thru – but every time they cried or whatever, everyone in the cinema laughed' (Lloyd 2008, 44). Not only does this scene invite critical reflection on fiction's ability to self-referentially comment on fictions. It explicitly references the sentimental fallacy by pointing out that 'tear-jerky' narratives can invite ridicule. It doesn't just *do* it, however, but requires a specific form of literacy that entails the willingness to acknowledge these references and in turn requires specific forms of literary-pedagogical training as well as a readiness to engage with literature productively and creatively.

It would be selling our own argument short if we remained only on the textual level without considering that literacy is what you make it in the learning group. *The Carbon Diaries 2015* provides ample opportunity for doing what our previous readings have suggested we look for in terms of discourse awareness, critical empathy, and socio-ecological complexities: The diary form *is* a helpful avenue for thinking about voice, authenticity, and discourse. The tableau of family members coping (or not) differently with the rationing regime provides a fruitful context for discussions (and the development) of critical empathy. Lastly, the novel offers a set of matter-of-fact comments that point to socio-ecological complexities when, for instance, Laura's friend Adi notes why the current catastrophe will receive more attention and incite more action than previous ones ('This ain't no New Orleans, this is rich white people getting killed. Everybody bothered now'; Lloyd 2008, 171), or when Laura and her gay neighbour discuss the potential of post-heteronormative 'carbon dating' (85–6). These affordances are for a whole learning group, who will find different elements of discourse important, empathise differently, and jointly create a richer tapestry of complexity than any individual reading would.

Notably, the text lends itself to challenging the fallacies we have been discussing above, too. This means and requires that teachers of literature are attentive to what can be seen as textual shortcomings as well and integrate those in appropriate task designs. One example is the much-lauded multimodality of this text (and others). Multimodality, as mentioned above, has been applauded for its authenticity, since 'multimodal texts have been omnipresent in our cultural and medial environment and everyday communication' (Hallet 2018, 27). This begs the question, however, if a single text should replicate such environments or whether it might be more rewarding to instead focus on a text's singular ability to step back from such communications and engage in its own ways of foregrounding, backgrounding, and staging real-world phenomena (climate change included). With the notion of texture, and through the suggestion to use text ensembles, the inclusive and multimodal potential of literary climate fictions is met differently, and by way of more than one text – which relieves the multimodal novel of offering more than its own narrativity for the sake of also duplicating other discourses. There are instances in *The Carbon Diaries 2015* in which multimodality might lead us dangerously close to the cognitive fallacy: It uses visuals and graphic design to sneak in climate and other facts, supposedly in a more interesting and appropriate form. One morning – Thursday, 2 April, as we learn – Laura waits for her best friend and thinks what a pain grown-ups are, when she – miraculously, one suspects – finds 'this piece of paper' that contains information on Greenland icecap melting, increased rainfall, and global change in oceanic salt levels. This might appear as a rather unsubtle attempt at sneaking in facts that could be better integrated in a more diversely textured text ensemble. But let us have a second look: In the case of the April note, the information is presented in tension with the overall narrative of love and desire and growing up because it has a note scribbled upon it – 'Ravi loves Thanz' – as well as a game of tic tac toe, thus showing how dramatic information about global environmental crisis is literally overwritten by garden-variety concerns of teenage love and boredom (see Lloyd 2008, 94). Hallet (2018, 33) rightly identifies such tensions as most productive, and we agree that they help us see that it would have been mistaken to assume climate change literacy improves just because of a different semiotic mode. Instead, that understanding is again brought about through ambiguity and complexity. As with other critical and affective engagements with literature, it is a matter of task design to ask the right questions of a text for teachers who seek to foster such understandings.

This clearly indicates that climate change literacy requires interdisciplinary exchange between literary studies and the educational sciences. It necessitates 'subject analysis' (that we have been exploring as literature environments), usually the strength of philological approaches, and the design of literacy environments, with useful suggestions coming from various strands of debate in education. Through a combination of both, climate change literacy can become instrumental in fostering more effective ways of tackling the gap between knowledge and action. Not in the sense of finally suggesting better ways of bringing about sustainable behaviour in learners, but in making a good case why the question has been posed wrongly all along.

Such a stance may help to also overcome '[o]verly narrow views of literature as a source of role models or moral precepts' that 'take insufficient account of the complexity of literary experience and literary texts, which often simultaneously challenge and reinforce traditional forms of thought and relations of power' (Lesnick 2006, 30). If 'literature is always a response to crisis, or an attempt to register its complexity', then we might want to pay better attention to the fact that there 'are as many forms of crisis as there are literary forms that can deliver insights into its processes' (Ahlberg 2021, 2). We also might want to register and counteract the individualistic and ultimately depoliticising tendency in educational models for environmental learning that individuals are asked to 'save the world' by simply moving into whichever kind of ecological action (Echterling 2016; Ideland 2019). This will require rethinking educational hopes in literary fiction as a 'catalyst for taking action' (Valente 2021). Even if literary reading, by virtue of literature's singularity and the potential of literacy events, offers unique access to interpreting crisis and to thus promoting change (cf. 4), we are convinced that its main achievements lie elsewhere. It fosters necessary skills and abilities, such as discourse awareness and competence, lacking in other disciplines concerned with climate and crisis (cf. Küchler 2017, 153; Bartosch 2020). Moreover, it offers new and critical ways for empathy and engaging with complexity as 'reading is characterized by a swing back and forth between myself as reader and the textual other in a process of continuous identification and disidentification' (Myren-Svelstad 2020, 7). This will result in action for sure – but this action is imaginative, communicative, collaborative and, ultimately, political.

Let us stay with this idea of swinging back and forth for a while longer and return to the concept of 'thinking twice' (see Section 1). We have suggested that understanding and engaging (climate) complexity emerges in the interplay of thinking both fast *and* slow when reading aesthetically and talking about texts and textures in meaningful tasks. If our thinking routinely operates in what Kahnemann calls System 1 and System 2 thinking – one fast and intuitive, the other slow and analytical – literary reading shows us that literature brings about a truly novel way of thinking in-between or in fact beyond the either-or scenario of these two systems. We suggest nothing less than that climate change literacy demands and engenders a System 3 way of thinking that oscillates between these two modes of thinking. Both fast thinking – aesthetic pleasure, the *qualia* of text and texture, and the entanglement of climate and other issues within the rich and ambiguous space of literary writing – *and* slow forms of thought that we are cultivating in interpretation, literary criticism and analysis, and 'slow reading' (Garrard 2010) – are integral to climate change literacy and, indeed, to any meaningful form of 'crisis education' (Kidman and Chang 2020). As thinking twice cultivates both sudden aesthetic apprehension and slower-paced contemplation, it brings about a climate change literacy whose objective is not in superficial behavioural change but in thickening understanding and in acting in language.

This is a way of grasping the unique potential of literary fiction in climate action and quality education contexts, as essentially every literary text asks us to 'think twice'. Being professional readers and educators, we know that every text warrants a second, closer look as well as an overall attention to its complex totality. As literate readers, we are moving back and forth between these modes of apprehension – but we are well advised to make this move-ment a central learning objective for those still in the process of finding their feet in the practice field of literature. Learning with climate fiction and becoming climate-change literate invites 'thinking twice': If we ever needed an argument for the role of literature and reading, and for a better understand-ing and deeper mutual recognition of the expertise in literary studies and literature pedagogy, it is based on this insight. It also entails realising that climate change literacy, as a capability and practice thriving on literature and moving beyond the sciences, requires and cultivates this third form of think-ing germane to literary reading.

Afterword: Climate Change Literacy Beyond Cli-Fi

Literary reading can play an integral part in cultivating climate change literacy and in thickening our understanding of climate change. As we have shown in this Element, the case of literature, however, needs to be made slightly differ-ently, especially regarding the idea that reading a book may effect desirable behavioural change. We have tried to provide arguments for this conviction – particularly by way of what we have proposed as the cognitive and sentimental fallacies and by underlining literature's insights into socio-ecological complex-ity through discourse awareness and critical empathy. And we have outlined what we think matters in educational contexts designed for fostering climate change literacy: the interplay of texts, textures, and tasks.

All the while, we have been keenly aware of the limitations of our own approach, especially regarding the corpus of texts we have been looking at.

True, these texts are doing very different things, and our argument has been concerned with the idea that a case can be made for such literary diversity, which by implication leaves space for other texts and different media. At the same time, we see their relative homogeneity – as cli-fi, as novels from the western hemisphere, and as writing coming from a specific temporal and cultural position. In the spirit of thinking twice, let us therefore in conclusion return to the idea of textual variety and probe the idea of climate change literacy beyond the specimens of cli-fi under scrutiny so far.

An obvious and indeed much-needed move would be towards non-Western perspectives. Novels such as American-Nigerian writer Nnedi Okorafor's *Lagoon* (2014), Aboriginal Australian author Alexis Wright's *Carpentaria* (2006) and *The Swan Book* (2013), or Indian-born novelist Amitav Ghosh's *Gun Island* (2019), besides being wonderful reads, offer 'radically different socio-climatic imaginaries' that help in 'challenging dominant, Eurocentric and restrictive ways of imagining the future', as Carl Death (2022, 432) demands (see also Streeby 2018). If climate change is a thoroughly cultured phenomenon, it goes without saying that cultural diversity is an asset when trying to understand its numerous ways of culturing; what is more, it makes a difference whether or not voices are heard that come from or engage with areas that are affected differently, and more often than not more dramatically, by climate change. Questions of responsibility and guilt, but also of hope and transformation, are posed and answered differently (Bartosch 2015), and such narratives may help to counter the tendency of some cli-fi (as well as much public debate on climate action) to 'erase Indigenous peoples' perspectives on the connection between climate change and colonial violence' (Whyte 2018, 225).

A reconsideration of fictions of climate change would also have to move beyond the currently dominant generic conventions that shape readerly expectations. It has been argued time and again that climate change is so complex and multifaceted that it becomes unnarratable. Nevertheless, and for better or worse, certain narrative patterns *have* developed that enable us to define cli-fi in the first place, including the occasionally problematic thematic focus on 'ice over heat, flood over drought, depopulated landscapes over demographic growth, and scarce resources over excessive consumption', as Ursula Heise puts it (2020, 495). Many alternatives to this exist and are currently in the making. Other modes and ways of contemporary storytelling engage with the climate question in ways that can further diversify the textures of climate change literacy: Charlotte McConaghy's 2020 novel *Migrations*, for instance, like many other recent texts focuses less on dramatic or apocalyptic climate catastrophes or future scenarios but is set in the present or very-near future and concentrates on issues of loss and mourning. Other texts, including Jenny Offill's *Weather* (2020) or Sarah Moss's

Summerwater (2020), do not adhere to any generic formula of the popular cli-fi canon but nonetheless seem to us indispensable for present-day climate fiction. The same is true for texts that focus on or explicitly include biodiversity and political crises, thus offering even more in terms of socio-ecological complexity (Ned Beauman's 2022 novel *Venomous Lumpsucker* or John Lanchester's *The Wall*, from 2019, to name but two recent examples).

Finally, readers and educators are well advised to eventually move beyond the novel form. As we have argued in the first section, our focus on novelistic narratives has mostly been a pragmatic decision, but we fully acknowledge that different media have different affordances and that textures ought to include those. A film such as *Take Shelter* (Dir. Jeff Nichols 2012), a play like Stephen Carleton's *The Turquoise Elephant* (2016), or an interactive poetry collection such as *Poem Forest* follows different rules of immersion and attention and therefore adds valuable new facets to climate change literacy as discussed in this Element (see Hoydis 2021). Likewise, there exist computer games and apps (such as *Climate Trail* and *Cranky Uncle*) and other forms of collaborative storytelling educators should consider for their singularity and fit with the notion of diversified textures and tasks.

These are just three suggestions for how to move beyond the confines of the cli-fi corpus we have been concerned with here. The selection will in future be even greater for sure, for 'it seems increasingly likely that climate fiction will simply become fiction in the years to come, because savvy readers will eventually refuse to accept any imagined human future that doesn't account for the climate crisis in some way', as Bell puts it: 'Even novels focused primarily on other subjects will have to acknowledge climate change, at least as cultural context and backdrop; those that don't will run the risk of seeming increasingly irreal, regardless of how grounded their depictions of life might otherwise be' (2021, 109–10). The list of texts is growing constantly, as should our attention to the increasing opportunities to bring more and more diverse narratives to bear on climate change literacy, conceived as 'composite, complex, and open to constant change as our knowledge of ecological changes and the effects of human actions are constantly revised' (Myren-Svelstad 2020, 17). This, as Myren-Svelstad avers, 'is not a panacea against environmental disaster, but it does amount to one brick in the edifice of sustainability, and probably the one literature has the best chance of contributing to' (17).

Writers such as Bell have identified relevant trends and developments of cli-fi, including a move from what he calls 'problem narratives' and 'aftermath narratives' to 'solution narratives' (Kim Stanley Robinson's 2020 *The Ministry for the Future* would be an obvious example) and better recognition, in criticism and scholarship, of Afrofuturism and indigenous futurisms (Bell 2021, 104–9).

Rather than reiterate a story of progress and linear development, we suggest considering all these aspects and more, including multimedia, filmic, and graphic narratives, creative nonfiction, and even texts that students come up with themselves as integral parts of an emerging climate change literacy. These texts and their different affordances are needed for our collaborative efforts to learn, and to unlearn, our ways of looking at this heating world. As Carl Lavery says, it is ultimately less about making great (and inevitably unfounded) claims about art's efficacy and what the texts 'do'; rather, it will always resemble more of 'an "undoing," a coming to terms with weakness and inadequacy' (Lavery 2018, 5). Climate change literacy, as we understand it, is about facing one's weaknesses and realising that some key questions about the role of literature have been wrongly put from the outset; it is also about recognising discursive, affective, and other complexities, and it is, ultimately, about thinking twice about language and meaning. The single text may give voice to inadequacies and refrain from presenting solutions, but it is nevertheless a 'brick in the edifice of sustainability'. We all, readers, educators, learners, are architects of this edifice, its millions of windows, hallways, and staircases – so let's get it ready for the difficult times to come.

References

Ahlberg, Sofia (2021). *Teaching Literature in Times of Crisis.* Routledge. https://doi.org/10.4324/9781003120742.

Ameel, Lieven (2021). 'Fraught Fictionality in Narratives of Future Catastrophe'. *Narrative* 29.3: 355–73. https://doi.org/10.1353/nar.2021.0022.

Attridge, Derek (2004). *The Singularity of Literature.* Routledge. https://doi.org/10.4324/9781315172477.

Atwood, Margaret (2015). 'It's Not Climate Change – It's Everything Change'. *Medium*, 27 July. https://medium.com/matter/it-s-not-climate-change-it-s-everything-change-8fd9aa671804.

Bacigalupi, Paolo (2009). *The Windup Girl.* Night Shade Books.

Bal, P. Matthijs and Martijn Veltkamp (2013). 'How Does Fiction Reading Influence Empathy? An Experimental Investigation on the Role of Emotional Transportation'. *PLoS ONE* 8.1: e55341, 1–12. https://doi.org/10.1371/journal.pone.0055341.

Barad, Karen (2000). 'Reconceiving Scientific Literacy as Agential Literacy: Or, Learning How to Intra-act Responsibly within the World'. In *Doing Science + Culture.* Ed. Roddey Reid and Sharon Traweek. Routledge, 221–58. https://doi.org/10.4324/9780203699256.

Bartosch, Roman (2015). 'The Climate of Literature: English Studies in the Anthropocene'. *Anglistik – International Journal of English Studies* 26.2: 59–70. https://angl.winter-verlag.de/article/ANGL/2015/2/6?_locale=en.

Bartosch, Roman (2017). 'Æsthetic Æffect: Relationality as a Core Concept in Environmental Studies and Education'. In *Ecocriticism – Environments in Anglophone Literatures.* Ed. Sonja Frenzel and Birgit Neumann. Winter, 33–57.

Bartosch, Roman (2018). 'Scale, Climate Change, and the Pedagogic Potential of Literature: Scaling (in) the Work of Barbara Kingsolver and T.C. Boyle'. *Open Library of Humanities* 4.2: 26, 1–21. https://doi.org/10.16995/olh.337.

Bartosch, Roman (2019). *Literature, Pedagogy, and Climate Change. Text Models for a Transcultural Ecology.* Palgrave Macmillan.

Bartosch, Roman (2020). 'Reading and Teaching Fictions of Climate'. In *Research Handbook on Communicating Climate Change.* Ed. David C. Holmes and Lucy M. Richardson. Edward Elgar, 349–52. https://doi.org/10.4337/9781789900408.00050.

Bartosch, Roman (2021). 'Scaling Crises: Theories, Tasks and Topics for Transformative Sustainability Education in English'. In *Towards*

Transformative Literature Pedagogy. Ed. Roman Bartosch. Wissenschaftlicher Verlag Trier, 77–90.

Bartosch, Roman (2022). 'Agonalität als Aufgabe: Relativität und Bildung für Nachhaltigkeit in der inklusiven Englischdidaktik'. *Relativität und Bildung. Fachübergreifende Herausforderungen und fachspezifische Grenzen*. Ed. Carolin Führer et al. Waxmann, 179–91.

Bateson, Gregory [1972] (2000). *Steps to an Ecology of Mind*. Chicago University Press.

Beach, Richard, Jeff Share and Allen Webb (2017). *Teaching Climate Change to Adolescents: Reading, Writing, and Making a Difference*. Routledge. https://doi.org/10.4324/9781315276304.

Bell, Matt (2021). 'Climate Fictions: Future-Making Technologies'. In *The Cambridge Companion to Environmental Humanities*. Ed. Jeffrey Jerome Cohen and Stephanie Foote. Cambridge University Press, 100–13. https://doi.org/10.1017/9781009039369.009.

Bergthaller, Hannes (2018). 'Climate Change and Un-Narratability'. *Metaphora* 2: v-1–12. https://metaphorajournal.univie.ac.at/.

Bergthaller, Hannes (2021). 'Humans'. In *The Cambridge Companion to Literature and the Anthropocene*. Ed. John Parham. Cambridge University Press, 211–25. https://doi.org/10.1017/9781108683111.014.

Bilodeau, Chantal (2018). 'Introduction'. In *Where Is the Hope? An Anthology of Short Climate Change Plays*. Ed. Chantal Bilodeau. Centre for Sustainable Practice in the Arts, xv–xvi.

Bloome, David and Judith Green (2015). 'The Social and Linguistic Turns in Studying Language and Literacy'. In *The Routledge Handbook of Literacy Studies*. Ed. Jennifer Rowsell and Kate Pahl. Routledge, 19–34. https://doi.org/10.4324/9781315717647.

Bonneuil, Christophe and Jean-Baptiste Fessoz (2013). *The Shock of the Anthropocene. The Earth, History and Us*. Verso.

Booth, Wayne C. (1990). *The Company We Keep: An Ethics of Fiction*. University of California Press.

Bortolussi, Maria and Peter Dixon (1996). 'The Effects of Formal Training on Literary Reception'. *Poetics* 23: 471–87.

Boykoff, Maxwell (2019). *Creative (Climate) Communications: Productive Pathways for Science, Policy and Society*. Cambridge University Press. https://doi.org/10.1017/9781108164047.

Boyle, T. C. (2000). *A Friend of the Earth*. Penguin.

Brady, Amy (2019). 'Climate Fiction: A Special Issue'. *Guernica*, 4 March. www.guernicamag.com/climate-fiction/.

Brady, Amy (2020). 'An Interview with Author and Scholar Matthew Schneider-Mayerson'. *Artists & Climate Change*, 6 August. https://artistsand climatechange.com/2020/08/06/an-interview-with-author-and-scholar-mat thew-schneider-mayerson/.

Braidotti, Rosi (2013). *The Posthuman*. Polity Press.

Bruhn, Jørgen (2019). '"We're Doomed – Now What?": Transmediating Temporality Into Narrative Forms'. In *Transmediations: Communication Across Media Borders*. Ed. Niklas Salmose and Lars Elleström, Routledge, 217–34.

Brune, Carlo (2020). *Literarästhetische Literalität: Literaturvermittlung im Spannungsfeld von Kompetenzorientierung und Bildungsideal*. transcript.

Buell, Lawrence (2005). *The Future of Environmental Criticism: Environmental Crisis and Literary Imagination*. Blackwell.

Caracciolo, Marco (2022). *Contemporary Fiction and Climate Uncertainty: Narrating Unstable Futures*. Bloomsbury Academic. http://dx.doi.org/10.5040/9781350233928.

Carl, Mark-Oliver, Moritz Jörgens, Tina Schulze, and Cornelia Rosebrock (2020). 'Strategien von Studierenden im Umgang mit literarästhetischen Texten'. *Leseräume: Zeitschrift für Literalität in Schule und Forschung* 7.6: 49-64.

Carneiro, Roberto and Jean Gordon (2013). 'Warranting Our Future: Literacy and Literacies'. *European Journal of Education* 48.4: 476–97. https://doi.org/10.1111/ejed.12055.

Carroll, Noël (1990). *The Philosophy of Horror: Or, Paradoxes of the Heart*. Routledge. https://doi.org/10.4324/9780203361894.

Celis-Diez, Juan L., Javiera Díaz-Forestier, Marcela Márquez-Garcia, and Silvia Lazzarino (2016). 'Biodiversity Knowledge Loss in Children's Books and Textbooks'. *Frontiers in Ecology and the Environment* 14.8: 408–10. https://doi.org/10.1002/fee.1324.

Center, Yola (2020). *Beginning Reading: A Balanced Approach to Literacy Instruction during the First Three Years at School*. Routledge. https://doi.org/10.4324/9781003115014.

Chapman, Daniel A., Brian Lickel, and Ezra M. Markowitz (2017). 'Reassessing Emotion in Climate Change Communication'. *Nature Climate Change* 7.12: 850–2. https://doi.org/10.1038/s41558-017-0021-9.

Chakrabarty, Dipesh (2021). *The Climate of History in a Planetary Age*. University of Chicago Press.

Clark, Timothy (2012). 'Scale'. In *Telemorphosis: Theory in the Era of Climate Change*. Ed. Tom Cohen. Vol. 1. Open Humanities Press, 148–66. http://

openhumanitiespress.org/books/download/Cohen_2012_Telemorphosis.pdf.

Clark, Timothy (2015). *Ecocriticism on the Edge: The Anthropocene as a Threshold Concept*. Bloomsbury Academic.

Clark, Timothy (2019). *The Value of Ecocriticism*. Cambridge University Press.

Cohen, Stanley (2001). *States of Denial: Knowing about Atrocities and Suffering*. Polity Press/Blackwell.

Cole, Matthew Benjamin (2022). '"At the Heart of Human Politics": Agency and Responsibility in the Contemporary Climate Novel'. *Environmental Politics* 31.1: 132–51. https://doi.org/10.1080/09644016.2021.1902699.

COVID-HL Network (2021). 'Health literacy in times of COVID-19'. https://covid-hl.eu/.

Death, Carl (2022). 'Climate Fiction, Climate Theory: Decolonising Imaginations of Global Futures'. *Millennium: Journal of International Studies* 50.2: 430–55. https://doi.org/10.1177/03058298211063926.

Diehr, Bärbel and Jutta Rymarczyk, Eds. (2015). *Researching Literacy in a Foreign Language among Primary School Learners*. Peter Lang.

Eagleton, Terry (2013). *The Event of Literature*. Yale University Press.

Echterling, Clare (2016). 'How to Save the World and Other Lessons from Children's Environmental Literature'. *Children's Literature in Education* 47.4: 283–99. https://doi.org/10.1007/s10583-016-9290-6.

Eppelsheimer, Natalie, Uwe Küchler and Charlotte Melin (2015). 'Claiming the Language Ecotone. Translinguality, Resilience, and the Environmental Humanities'. *Resilience: A Journal of the Environmental Humanities* 1.3. https://doi.org/10.5250/resilience.1.3.005.

Evancie, Angela. 'Did climate change create a new literary genre?' 21 April 2013. https://narrativeblog.wordpress.com/2013/04/21/did-climate-change-create-a-new-literary-genre-angela-evancie/.

Felski, Rita (2008). *Uses of Literature*. Blackwell.

Feski, Rita (2020). *Hooked: Art and Attachment*. Chicago University Press.

Fialho, Olivia (2019). 'What is Literature for? The Role of Transformative Reading'. *Cogent Arts & Humanities* 6: 1692532. https://doi.org/10.1080/23311983.2019.1692532.

Fish, Stanley. ([1967] 1998). *Surprised by Sin: The Reader in* Paradise Lost. 2nd ed. Harvard University Press.

Garrard, Greg (2010). 'A Novel Idea: Slow Reading'. *Times Higher Education*, 17 June. www.timeshighereducation.com/news/a-novel-idea-slow-reading/412075.article

Garrard, Greg (2012a). *Ecocriticism*. 2nd ed. Routledge. https://doi.org/10.4324/9780203806838.

Garrard, Greg (2012b). 'Introduction'. In *Teaching Ecocriticism and Green Cultural Studies*. Ed. Greg Garrard. Palgrave Macmillan, 1–10. https://doi.org/10.1057/9780230358393.

Garrard, Greg (2013). '*Solar*: Apocalypse Not'. In *Ian McEwan: Contemporary Critical Perspectives*. Ed. Sebastian Groes. 2nd ed. Bloomsbury Academic, 123–35.

Garrard, Greg (2017). 'In-flight Behaviour: Teaching Climate Change Literature in First-Year Intro English'. In *Teaching Climate Change in the Humanities*. Ed. Stephen Siperstein, Shane Hall, and Stephanie LeMenager. Routledge, 118–25. https://doi.org/10.4324/9781315689135.

Garrard, Grey (2019). 'Never too soon, always too late: Reflections on Climate Temporality'. *WIREs Climate Change* 11.1: e605. https://doi.org/10.1002/wcc.605.

Garrard, Greg (2021). 'Cultivating Viewpoint Diversity in Ecocritical Pedagogy'. In *Cultivating Sustainability in Language and Literature Pedagogy. Steps to an Educational Ecology*. Ed. Roman Bartosch. Routledge, 47–63.

Garrard, Greg, Axel Goodbody, George Handley and Stephanie Posthumus (2019). *Climate Change Scepticism: A Transnational Ecocritical Analysis*. Bloomsbury Academic. https://doi.org/10.5040/9781350057050.

Garrard, Greg, Gary Handwerk and Sabine Wilke (2014). 'Introduction: Imagining Anew: Challenges of Representing the Anthropocene'. *Environmental Humanities* 5: 149–153.

Gee, James Paul (2015). 'The New Literacy Studies'. In *The Routledge Handbook of Literacy Studies*. Ed. Jennifer Rowsell and Kate Pahl. Routledge, 35–48.

Ghosh, Amitav (2016). *The Great Derangement: Climate Change and the Unthinkable*. University of Chicago Press.

Goodbody, Axel (2020). 'Beyond Communication: Climate Change Fiction'. In *Research Handbook on Communicating Climate Change*. Ed. David C. Holmes and Lucy M. Richardson. Edward Elgar, 320–9. https://doi.org/10.4337/9781789900408.00047.

Goodbody, Axel and Adeline Johns-Putra, eds. (2019). *Cli-Fi: A Companion*. Peter Lang. https://doi.org/10.3726/b12457.

Grabes, Herbert (2008). 'Prodesse et Delectare: The World of National Literatures and the World of Literature'. In *Re-Thinking Europe*. Ed. Nele Bemong, Mirjam Truwant, and Pieter Vermeulen. Brill, 209–21.

Gurr, Jens Martin (2010). 'Emplotting an Ecosystem: Amitav Ghosh's *The Hungry Tide* and the Question of Form in Ecocriticism'. In *Local Natures, Global Responsibilities: Ecocritical Perspectives on the New English*

Literatures. Ed. Laurenz Volkmann, Nancy Grimm, Ines Detmers, and Katrin Thomson. Rodopi, 69–80.

Hall, Shane Donnelly (2015). 'Learning to Imagine the Future: The Value of Affirmative Speculation in Climate Change Education'. *Resilience: A Journal of the Environmental Humanities* 2.2: 14.

Hallet, Wolfgang (2018). 'Reading Multimodal Fiction: A Methodological Approach'. *Anglistik: International Journal of English Studies* 29.1: 25–40. https://angl.winter-verlag.de/article/ANGL/2018/1/4?_locale=en.

Heise, Ursula K. (2020). 'Climate Crisis and Narrative Forecasting'. *Germanisch-Romanische Monatsschrift* 70.3–4: 495–507.

Hicks, David (2015). 'Learning to See Climate Change'. *Teaching Geography* 40.3: 94–6.

Hiser, Krista K. and Matthew K. Lynch (2021). 'Worry and Hope: What College Students Know, Think, Feel, and Do about Climate Change'. *Journal of Community Engagement and Scholarship* 13.3: 96–107. https://jces.ua.edu/articles/10.54656/IOWF3526.

Holmes, David C. and Lucy M. Richardson, Eds. (2020). *Research Handbook on Communicating Climate Change*. Edward Elgar.

Hoydis, Julia (2019). *Risk and the English Novel: From Defoe to McEwan*. De Gruyter. https://doi.org/10.1515/9783110615418.

Hoydis, Julia (2020). '(In)Attention and Global Drama: Climate Change Plays'. In *Research Handbook on Communicating Climate Change*. Ed. David C. Holmes and Lucy M. Richardson. Edward Elgar, 340–8.

Hoydis, Julia (2021). 'Literature and Interdisciplinary (Health) Risk Research: Of Boundary Objects, Thought Styles, and Narratives of Uncertainty'. *Anglistik: International Journal of English Studies* 32.3: 87–102. https://doi.org/10.33675/ANGL/2021/3/9.

Hufnagel, Elizabeth (2017). 'Attending to Emotional Expressions about Climate Change: A Framework for Teaching and Learning'. In *Teaching and Learning about Climate Change: A Framework for Educators*. Ed. Daniel P. Shepardson, Anita Roychoudhury and Andrew S. Hirsch. Routledge, 43–55. https://doi.org/10.4324/9781315629841.

Hulme, Mike (2010). *Why We Disagree about Climate Change: Understanding Controversy, Inaction and Opportunity*. 6th ed. Cambridge University Press. https://doi.org/10.1017/CBO9780511841200.

Hulme, Mike (2021). *Climate Change*. Routledge. https://doi.org/10.4324/9780367822675.

Ideland, Malin (2019). *The Eco-Certified Child: Citizenship and Education for Sustainability and Environment*. Palgrave Macmillan. https://doi.org/10.1007/978-3-030-00199-5.

Idema, Tom (2020). 'When the Levees Break: Global Heating, Watery Rhetoric and Complexity in Paolo Bacigalupi's *The Windup Girl'*. *Green Letters: Studies in Ecocriticism* 24.1: 51–63. https://doi.org/10.1080/14688417.2020.1752509.

Ismail, Sherif H. (2022) 'On Why Less is More in Climate Fiction'. *Interdisciplinary Studies in Literature and Environment*, isac057, https://doi.org/10.1093/isle/isac057.

James, Erin (2022). *Narrative in the Anthropocene*. Ohio State University Press.

James, Carl and Peter Garrett (1995). *Language awareness in the Classroom*. Longman.

Kagan, Sacha (2011). *Art and Sustainability: Connecting Patterns for a Culture of Complexity*. Transcript.

Kahneman, Daniel (2012). *Thinking, Fast and Slow*. Penguin.

Keen, Suzanne (2007). *Empathy and the Novel*. Oxford University Press.

Kepser, Matthis and Ulf Abraham (2016). *Literaturdidaktik Deutsch: Eine Einführung*. 4th ed. Erich Schmidt Verlag.

Kerridge, Richard (2010). 'The Single Source [on *Solar*]'. *Ecozon@* 1.1: 155–61. https://doi.org/10.37536/ECOZONA.2010.1.1.334.

Kidman, Gillian, and Chew-Hung Chang (2020). 'What does "crisis education" look like?' *International Research in Geographical and Environmental Education* 29.2: 107–11.

Kingsolver, Barbara (2012). *Flight Behavior*. Harper.

Klöckner, Christian A. (2020). 'Communication to Change Climate-related Behaviour'. In *Research Handbook on Communicating Climate Change*. Ed. David C. Holmes and Lucy M. Richardson. Edward Elgar, 116–25.

Kollmuss, Anja and Julian Agyeman (2002). 'Mind the Gap: Why Do People Act Environmentally and What Are the Barriers to Pro-Environmental Behavior?' *Environmental Education Research* 8.3: 239–60. https://doi.org/10.1080/13504620220145401.

Kössinger, Nobert and Claudia Wittig (2019). 'Prodesse et delectare – An Introduction'. In *Prodesse et delectare. Case Studies on Didactic Literature in the European Middle Ages*. Ed. Norbert Kössinger and Claudia Wittig. De Gruyter, 1–12. https://doi.org/10.1515/9783110650068-001.

Küchler, Uwe (2017). 'Signs, Images, and Narratives: Climate Change across Languages and Cultures'. In *Teaching Climate Change in the Humanities*. Ed. Stephen Siperstein, Shane Hall, and Stephanie LeMenager. Routledge, 153–60. https://doi.org/10.4324/9781315689135.

Lakoff, George (2004). *Don't Think of an Elephant! Know Your Values and Frame the Debate: The Essential Guide for Progressives*. Chelsea Green.

Lavery, Carl (2018). 'Introduction: Performance and Ecology – What Can Theatre Do?' In *Performance and Ecology: What Can Theatre Do?* Ed. Carl Lavery. Routledge, 1–9.

Lehtimäki, Markku (2020). 'A Comedy of Survival: Narrative Progression and the Rhetoric of Climate Change in Ian McEwan's *Solar*'. In *Environment and Narrative: New Directions in Econarratology*. Ed. Erin James and Eric Morel. Ohio State University Press, 87–105.

Lesnick, Alice (2006). 'Forms of Engagement: The Ethical Significance of Literacy Teaching'. *Ethics and Education* 1.1: 29–45. https://doi.org/10.1080/17449640600584953.

Lloyd, Saci (2008). *The Carbon Diaries 2015*. Holiday House.

Mączyńska, Magdalena (2023). 'Attention, Connection, Dialogue: Teaching Barbara Kingsolver's *Flight Behavior* in the Climate Fiction Classroom'. In *Teaching the Literature of Climate Change*. Ed. Debra J. Rosenthal. MLA.

Maggs, David and John Robinson (2020). *Sustainability in an Imaginary World: Art and the Question of Agency*. Routledge. https://doi.org/10.4324/9780429346583.

Marks, Elizabeth, et al. (2021). 'Young People's Voices on Climate Anxiety, Government Betrayal and Moral Injury: A Global Phenomenon'. *The Lancet*, 7 September. http://dx.doi.org/10.2139/ssrn.3918955.

Martínez, María-Ángeles (2018). *Storyworld Possible Selves*. De Gruyter. https://doi.org/10.1515/9783110571028.

Massumi, Brian (2008). 'The Thinking-Feeling of What Happens: A Semblance of a Conversation'. *3 Inflexions* 1.1 'How Is Research-Creation?' www.inflexions.org.

Matthewman, Sasha (2011). *Teaching Secondary English as if the Planet Matters*. Routledge. https://doi.org/10.4324/9780203834534.

Mauch, Christof (2019). *Slow Hope: Rethinking Ecologies of Crisis and Fear*. Rachel Carson Center. https://doi.org/10.5282/rcc/8556.

McEwan, Ian (2010). *Solar*. Jonathan Cape.

McKibben, Bill (2011). 'Introduction'. In *I'm with the Bears: Short Stories from a Damaged Planet*. Ed. Mark Martin. Verso, 1–5.

Milkoreit, Manjana (2016). 'The Promise of Climate Fiction: Imagination, Storytelling, and the Politics of the Future'. In *Reimagining Climate Change*. Ed. Paul Wapner and Hilal Elver. Routledge, 71–191. https://doi.org/10.4324/9781315671468.

Miller, J. Hillis (2005). *Literature as Conduct: Speech Acts in Henry James*. Fordham University Press.

Moore, Michele-Lee and Manjana Milkoreit (2020). 'Imagination and Transformations to Sustainable and Just Futures'. *Elementa: Science of the Anthropocene* 8.1: 081, 1–17. https://doi.org/10.1525/elementa.2020.081.

Morton, Timothy (2013). *Hyperobjects: Philosophy and Ecology after the End of the World*. University of Minnesota Press.

Moser, Susanne C. (2010). 'Communicating Climate Change: History, Challenges, Process and Future Directions'. *WIREs Climate Change* 1.1: 31–53. https://doi.org/10.1002/wcc.11.

Myren-Svelstad, Per Esben (2020). 'Sustainable Literary Competence: Connecting Literature Education to Education for Sustainability'. *Humanities* 9.4: 141, 1–19. https://doi.org/10.3390/h9040141.

Naqvi, Rahat (2015). 'Postcolonial Approaches to Literacy: Understanding the "Other"'. In *The Routledge Handbook of Literacy Studies*. Ed. Jennifer Rowsell and Kate Pahl. Routledge, 49–61. https://doi.org/10.4324/9781315717647.

Nikoleris, Alexandra, Johannes Stripple and Paul Tenngart (2017). 'Narrating Climate Futures: Shared Socioeconomic Pathways and Literary Fiction'. *Climatic Change* 143: 307–19. https://doi.org/10.1007/s10584-017-2020-2.

Norgaard, Kari Marie (2011). *Living in Denial: Climate Change, Emotions, and Everyday Life*. MIT Press. https://doi.org/10.7551/mitpress/9780262015448 .001.0001.

Oreskes, Naomi (2004). 'The Scientific Consensus on Climate Change'. *Science* 306.5702: 1686. https://doi.org/10.1126/science.1103618.

Ortiz Robles, Mario (2010). *The Novel as Event*. University of Michigan Press. https://doi.org/10.3998/mpub.1825347.

Otto, Ilona M., et al. (2020). 'Social Tipping Dynamics for Stabilizing Earth's Climate by 2050'. *PNAS* 117.5: 2354–65. https://doi.org/10.1073/ pnas.1900577117

Parham, John (2006). 'The Deficiency of "Environmental Capital": Why Environmentalism Needs a Reflexive Pedagogy'. In *Ecodidactic Perspectives of English Language, Literatures and Cultures*. Ed. Sylvia Mayer and Graham Wilson. WVT, 7–22.

Pearce, Warren et al. (2017). 'Beyond Counting Climate Consensus'. *Environmental Communication* 11:6, 723–30. https://doi.org/10.1080/ 17524032.2017.1333965.

Plantinga, Carl (1999). 'The Scene of Empathy and the Human Face on Film'. In *Passionate Views: Film, Cognition, and Emotion*. Ed. Carl Plantinga and Greg M. Smith. Johns Hopkins University Press, 239–55.

Plumwood, Val (2002). 'Decolonising Relationships with Nature'. *PAN: Philosophy Activism Nature* 2: 7–30. https://doi.org/10.4225/03/57D8A6217 7281.

Puchner, Martin. (2022). *Literature for a Changing Planet*. Princeton University Press.

Reinfandt, Christoph (2013). '"Texture" as a Key Term in Literary and Cultural Studies'. In *Text or Context: Reflections on Literary and Cultural Criticism*. Ed. Rüdiger Kunow and Stephan Mussil. Königshausen & Neumann, 7–21.

Reinfandt, Christoph (2020). 'Text als Angebot: Didaktische Perspektiven nach der Literaturtheorie'. In *Theorien! Horizonte für die Lehrerinnen- und Lehrerbildung*. Ed. Martin Harant, Philipp Thomas and Uwe Küchler. Tübingen University Press, 449–63. http://dx.doi.org/10.15496/publikation-45627.

Rich, Nathaniel (2013). *Odds Against Tomorrow*. Farrar, Straus and Giroux.

Robinson, Kim Stanley (2004). *Forty Signs of Rain*. Bantam.

Rosenblatt, Louise M. (1978). *The Reader, the Text, the Poem*. Southern Illinois University Press.

Schneider-Mayerson, Matthew (2018). 'The Influence of Climate Fiction: An Empirical Survey of Readers'. *Environmental Humanities* 10.2: 473–500. https://doi.org/10.1215/22011919-7156848.

Schneider-Mayerson, Matthew (2019). 'Whose Odds? The Absence of Climate Justice in American Climate Fiction Novels'. *ISLE* 26.4: 944–67. https://doi.org/10.1093/isle/isz081.

Schneider-Mayerson, Matthew (2020). '"Just as in the Book'? The Influence of Literature on Readers' Awareness of Climate Injustice and Perception of Climate Migrants'. *ISLE* 27.2: 337–64. https://doi.org/10.1093/isle/isaa020.

Schneider-Mayerson, Matthew, et al. (2020). 'Environmental Literature as Persuasion: An Experimental Test of the Effects of Reading Climate Fiction'. *Environmental Communication* 17.1: 1–16. https://doi.org/10.1080/17524032.2020.1814377.

Schneidewind, Uwe (2013). 'Wandel verstehen: Auf dem Weg zu einer "Transformative Literacy"'. In *Wege aus der Wachstumsgesellschaft*. Ed. Harald Welzer and Klaus Wiegandt. Fischer, 115–40.

Seilman, Uffe and Steen F. Larsen (1989). 'Personal Resonance to Literature: A Study of Remindings while Reading'. *Poetics* 18.1–2: 165–77. https://doi.org/10.1016/0304-422X(89)90027-2.

Shepardson, Daniel P., Anita Roychoudhury and Andrew S. Hirsch, Eds. (2017). *Teaching and Learning about Climate Change: A Framework for Educators*. Routledge. https://doi.org/10.4324/9781315629841.

Siperstein, Stephen, Shane Hall, and Stephanie LeMenager (2017). 'Introduction'. In *Teaching Climate Change in the Humanities*. Ed. Stephen Siperstein, Shane Hall, and Stephanie LeMenager. Routledge, 1–13. https://doi.org/10.4324/9781315689135.

Slovic, Scott (2017). 'The Elephant in the Room: Acknowledging Global Climate Change in Courses Not Focused on Climate'. In *Teaching Climate Change in the Humanities*. Ed. Stephen Siperstein, Shane Hall, and Stephanie LeMenager. Routledge, 163–9. https://doi.org/10.4324/9781315689135.

Smith, Joe (2011). 'Why Climate Change is Different: Six Elements that are Shaping the New Cultural Politics'. In *Culture and Climate Change*. Ed. Robert Butler, Joe Smith, and Renata Tyszczuk. Shed, 17–22. https://citizen joesmith.wordpress.com/2012/02/15/why-climate-change-is-different-six-elements-that-are-shaping-the-new-cultural-politics/.

Smith, Philip and Nicolas Howe (2015). *Climate Change as Social Drama: Global Warming in the Public Sphere*. Cambridge University Press. https:// doi.org/10.1017/CBO9781316217269.

Snaza, Nathan (2019). *Animate Literacies: Literature, Affect, and the Politics of Humanism*. Duke University Press. https://doi.org/10.1215/9781478005629.

Spivak, Gayatri Chakravorty (2012). *An Aesthetic Education in the Era of Globalisation*. Harvard University Press.

Stables, Andrew (2006). 'On Teaching and Learning the Book of the World'. In *Ecodidactic Perspectives in English* Language, *Literatures*. Ed. Sylvia Mayer and Graham Wilson. WVT, 145–62.

Stengers, Isabelle (2015). *In Catastrophic Times: Resisting the Coming Barbarism*. Trans. Andrew Goffey. Open Humanities Press. http://openhuma nitiespress.org/books/download/Stengers_2015_In-Catastrophic-Times.pdf.

Sterling, Andrew (2010). 'Keep it Complex'. *Nature* 468, 1029–31. https://doi .org/10.1038/4681029a.

Stibbe, Arran and Heather Luna (2009). 'Introduction'. In *The Handbook of Sustainability Literacy: Skills for a Changing World*. Ed. Arran Stibbe. Green Books, 9–16.

Stockwell, Peter (2012). *Texture: A Cognitive Aesthetics of Reading*. Edinburgh University Press.

Streeby, Shelley (2018). *Imagining the Future of Climate Change: World-Making through Science Fiction and Activism*. University of California Press. https://doi.org/10.1525/9780520967557.

'Tanya'. 'Review- *Friend of the Earth'*. *Goodreads.com* 3 June 2000. www .goodreads.com/review/show/3373477147.

UNESCO (2017). 'Education for Sustainable Development Goals: Learning Objectives'. https://unesdoc.unesco.org/ark:/48223/pf0000247444.

US Global Change Research Program (2009). *Climate Literacy: The Essential Principles of Climate Science. A Guide for Individuals and Communities*. www.climate.gov/teaching/essential-principlesclimate-literacy/essential-principles-climate-literacy.

Valente, David (2021). 'Recommended Reads: Environmental Children's Literature – A Catalyst for Taking Action'. *Children's Literature in English Language Education* 9.1: 1–11. https://clelejournal.org/introduced-david-valente/.

van der Linden, Sander, Anthony Leiserowitz, and Edward W. Maibach (2017). 'Gateway Illusion or Cultural Cognition Confusion?'. *Journal of Science Communication* 16.5: A04, 1–24. http://dx.doi.org/10.2139/ssrn.3094256.

van Holt, Nadine and Norbert Groeben (2005). 'Das Konzept des Foregrounding in der modernen Textverarbeitungspsychologie'. *Journal für Psychologie* 13.4: 311–32. https://nbn-resolving.org/urn:nbn:de:0168-ssoar-17132.

Vermeule, Blakey (2010). *Why Do We Care About Literary Characters?* Johns Hopkins University Press.

Volkmann, Laurenz (2010). *Fachdidaktik Englisch: Kultur und Sprache.* Narr.

Volkmann, Laurenz (2015). 'Literary Literacy and Intercultural Competence: Furthering Students Knowledge, Skills, and Attitudes'. In *Learning with Literature in the EFL Classroom*, Ed. Werner Delanoy and Maria Eisenmann, and Frauke Matz, Peter Lang. 49–66.

Vraga, Emily and Sander van der Linden (2020). 'Responding to Climate Science Denial'. In *Research Handbook on Communicating Climate Change*, Ed. David C. Holmes and Lucy M. Richardson. Edward Elgar, 79–91. https://doi.org/10.4337/9781789900408.00015

Weik von Mossner, Alexa (2017a). *Affective Ecologies: Empathy, Emotion, and Environmental Narrative.* Ohio State University Press.

Weik von Mossner, Alexa (2017b). 'Vulnerable Lives: The Affective Dimensions of Risk in Young Adult Cli-Fi'. *Textual Practice* 31.3: 553–66. https://doi.org/10.1080/0950236X.2017.1295661

Welzer, Harald (n.d.). Interview by Tim Turiak 'Man muss ein bisschen Remmidemmi machen'. *Die letzten Menschen: Kulturmagazin.* http://dieletztenmenschen.com/interview/man-muss-ein-bisschen-remmidemmi-machen/

Whyte, Kyle P. (2018). 'Indigenous Science (Fiction) for the Anthropocene: Ancestral Dystopias and Fantasies of Climate Change Crises'. *Environment and Planning E: Nature and Space* 1.1–2: 224–42. https://doi.org/10.1177/2514848618777621.

Zapf, Hubert (2016). *Literature as Cultural Ecology. Sustainable Texts.* Bloomsbury.

Zarcadoolas, Christina, Andrew F. Pleasant, and David S. Greer (2006). *Advancing Health Literacy: A Framework for Understanding and Action.* Jossey-Bass.

Acknowledgements

This Element is the result of a project generously funded by the Volkswagen Foundation. For all her help and support we thank Barbara Neubauer. In the writing process, we have benefitted greatly from discussions with our 'critical friends' Jan Alber, Wiebke Dannecker, and Julika Griem. The same is true of conversations with Kate Rigby, Director of MESH – Multidisciplinary Environmental Studies in the Humanities – at the University of Cologne, who is not only inspiring to work with but has provided helpful comments on a draft version of our text. We are also grateful to Serenella Iovino, Louise Westling, and Timo Maran, editors of the Cambridge Elements in the Environmental Humanities series, for accepting this volume for the series. Moreover, the comments of three anonymous reviewers helped us to improve the manuscript. Heartfelt thanks to our excellent student assistants Paula Dierkes, Svenja Donner, and Annika Steffens for help with research tasks and with preparing the final manuscript for print, also to Elisabeth Haefs for proofreading. In this project, as in so many others, Christine Cangemi at the University of Duisburg-Essen has been a pragmatic and circumspect financial administrator, as has been Marie Eicker at the University of Cologne. Moreover, we are grateful for numerous opportunities to present our work and discuss our ideas with the organisers and participants of various events, including the colloquium of the Cologne Centre for Language Sciences, the literacies.net lecture series (Essen and Cincinnati), the 'Narratives and Metaphors of Sustainability' symposium (Bochum), the KWI 'Ecologies of Fear' workshop, the University of Cologne's 'Global Environmental Humanities' lecture series, the European UNITE Summer School 'Sustainability in Schools and Teacher Education', and the UDE4Future group. We particularly wish to thank Nassim W. Balestrini, Achim Daschkeit, Julie Doyle, Greg Garrard, David Higgins, Kirk Junker, Bernd Sommer, Warren Pearce, Carolin Schwegler, and Harald Welzer for contributing inspiring talks to our online lecture series 'Perspectives on Climate Change Communication' during the summer term of 2022, organised as part of the Wissenschaftsforum zu Köln und Essen. We thank its director, Wilfried Hinsch, for his generous support and Ursula K. Heise for joining our project group 'Cultures of Climate' as first Visiting Professor for Public Humanities in October 2022. We dedicate this Element to all pupils and students, educators and scholars who are making a difference. Funded by the Volkswagen Foundation.

Cambridge Elements ☰

Environmental Humanities

Louise Westling
University of Oregon

Louise Westling is an American scholar of literature and environmental humanities who was a founding member of the Association for the Study of Literature and Environment and its President in 1998. She has been active in the international movement for environmental cultural studies, teaching and writing on landscape imagery in literature, critical animal studies, biosemiotics, phenomenology, and deep history.

Serenella Iovino
University of North Carolina at Chapel Hill

Serenella Iovino is Professor of Italian Studies and Environmental Humanities at the University of North Carolina at Chapel Hill. She has written on a wide range of topics, including environmental ethics and ecocritical theory, bioregionalism and landscape studies, ecofeminism and posthumanism, comparative literature, eco-art, and the Anthropocene.

Timo Maran
University of Tartu

Timo Maran is an Estonian semiotician and poet. Maran is Professor of Ecosemiotics and Environmental Humanities and Head of the Department of Semiotics at the University of Tartu. His research interests are semiotic relations of nature and culture, Estonian nature writing, zoosemiotics and species conservation, and semiotics of biological mimicry.

About the Series

The environmental humanities is a new transdisciplinary complex of approaches to the embeddedness of human life and culture in all the dynamics that characterize the life of the planet. These approaches reexamine our species' history in light of the intensifying awareness of drastic climate change and ongoing mass extinction. To engage this reality, Cambridge Elements in Environmental Humanities builds on the idea of a more hybrid and participatory mode of research and debate, connecting critical and creative fields.

Cambridge Elements

Environmental Humanities

Elements in the Series

A full series listing is available at: www.cambridge.org/EIEH

Printed in the United States
by Baker & Taylor Publisher Services